What are Others Saying about This Book?

At a time in business when the most prized economic currency is information and knowledge, it should be on every leader's agenda to read this book. Rodger's thorough presentation of the Corporate Intelligence 'engine' will give business readers the tools by which to harness and institutionalize this currency into every day organizational life while avoiding the common trap of information overload. In our industry, where the "assets" go home each night (and take knowledge with them), getting this right is crucial.
Michael Shostak,
Executive Vice-President, Managing Director - Interactive
Arnold Worldwide Canada

This material contains powerful information gathering and processing tools to empower the workforce in driving sustainable business.
Stephanie Mackendrick,
President,
Canadian Women in Communications (CWC-AFC)

Rodger is an energetic, entertaining and a highly educational facilitator. I would strongly recommend his Corporate Intelligence Awareness program.
Barry Mackinnon,
VP Marketing,
Bombardier Aerospace

This material is an invaluable resource to any organization intent on enhancing an efficient information/intelligence culture.
Mike Ferreira,
Director Communications,
BBM Canada

Corporate Intelligence Awareness

Securing the Competitive Edge

By Rodger Nevill Harding, B.A., LLB

Multi-Media Publications Inc.

Lakefield, Ontario

Corporate Intelligence Awareness: Securing the Competitive Edge

By Rodger Nevill Harding

Published by:
Multi-Media Publications Inc.
R.R. #4B, Lakefield, Ontario, Canada, K0L 2H0

http://www.mmpubs.com/

ISBN-10 (hardcover edition):   1-895186-42-0
ISBN-13 (hardcover edition):   9781895186420
ISBN-10 (Adobe PDF ebook edition):   1-895186-43-9
ISBN-13 (Adobe PDF ebook edition):   9781895186437

First printing 2005.
Printed in the USA and Great Britain. Published in Canada.

Library and Archives Canada Cataloguing in Publication

Harding, Rodger Nevill
        Corporate intelligence awareness : securing the competitive edge / by Rodger Nevill Harding.

ISBN 1-895186-42-0 (bound).--ISBN 1-895186-43-9 (Adobe PDF ebook)

1. Business intelligence. I. Title.

HD38.7.H365 2006   658.4'72   C2006-904052-4

Contents

Acknowledgements

My thanks to N.H., N.E. and M-L.H. for the inspiration and sustenance that made this book possible.

Dedication

This book is dedicated to forward thinkers – You give true meaning to creativity and innovation.

Introduction

Prompted by corporate clients, this material has evolved from a seminar workbook to a one-stop handbook that will assist corporations in the creation or enhancement of a dynamic and viable intelligence/knowledge culture that will increase efficiency and bottom line business objectives.

My preoccupation with *real* intelligence is largely in reaction to those companies that equate intelligence with Competitive Intelligence (CI) tools and the technical storage, cross-referencing and processing of available information rather than an accumulation of clues that form a theory or predict a future event. Compliance with a cut and paste information gathering process will not be as effective as the creation of a unique, knowledge culture that will use all available human capital **and** technology to the fullest, resulting in maximum profit levels.

In the pursuit of sustaining distinct and effective information and knowledge policy implementation, there are three basic themes that the reader will be asked repeatedly to explore in the pages to come:

- Raising thinking about intelligence to conscious levels will result in the required awareness to remain informed, strategic and flexible. In a changing world this is not easy - the constant evaluation and re-evaluation of readily available information, people and situations has never been more crucial. A conscious effort is required to overcome individual and organizational barriers that inhibit innovative decision-making processes.

- Leadership in the intelligence world is the conscious decision of the individual to accept the responsibility of a unique role as protector of corporate assets as well as the gatherer, processor and deliverer of vital information.

- The Protection of Assets is an ongoing task that requires the loyalty, dedication and vigilance of all employees. If organizational uniqueness is recognized as the corporation's strongest asset, then (of necessity) a daily awareness of the importance of protecting, gathering and processing information will mean a corresponding awareness of *what walks out the door.*

For those who feel that creative thinking, objective setting, intuition, managing uncertainty and relationship building are fuzzy topics, it is hoped that the following pages will show that these realities underpin the very survival of an organization.

The information highway with the ongoing IT revolution allows people, within minutes, to access just about anything that has been published. Analyzing and translating available material into expedient policy is the challenge; it is this competency that will secure foreknowledge of industry trends, enhancing the ability to make informed decisions and so provide the competitive edge.

Ethics, Legality & The World Of Intelligence Gathering

This material is designed to make conscious the role of the individual in the protection, collection and processing of information in the corporate world and will discuss methods to ensure the awareness and analysis of facts, data and available information.

To ignore this vast resource would be unnatural. Be sure that those who access this information will be informed and current - informed employees will allow the companies they represent a chance at enhancing or maintaining a competitive advantage in their respective fields.

Ethics and legality are dynamic, value-driven concepts that differ from person to person, organization to organization, town to town, country to country, and situation to situation! These differences will of necessity dictate varied interpretation styles.

The author's guidelines:

- It is generally not considered **ethical** to cultivate and establish relationships and contacts for the sole purpose of gathering information.

Professional spies engage in this activity - it is called corporate espionage. Hopefully, a mercenary approach to relationships in the intelligence gathering process would be abhorrent to you, the reader

- The invasion of a private or corporate/ organizational space for the purpose of discovering information is **illegal** in most countries. In recent years, the growing emphasis placed on **Intellectual Property** and its legal protection has widened the interpretation of what constitutes space and property. Most large corporations will have access to legal opinion in this regard. It is suggested that an empathetic approach of *doing unto others as you would have done to yourself,* would be the safest rule of thumb to follow.

What is Intelligence?

Intelligence is foreknowledge of something that has not yet happened. Intelligence describes the product that results from *thinking* about what is likely to happen –an accumulation of subjectively-discovered clues that will form an objective theory or predict a future event. An Intelligence Theory is the special ingredient in policy/ planning/strategic initiatives that is exclusive to a particular organization at any point in time. Once intelligence *happens* it becomes information or data and is generally available to all interested parties.

Good intelligence input results in effective business practice and increased profits. Each employee has a vital role to play in sustaining the intelligence flow. Ensuring that the individual is *consciously* aware of available information, informed as to corporate objectives, and capable of evolving a personal knowledge management strategy, the first cycle of the intelligence process is complete. All that remains is to tap into this wealth of readily available intelligence.

Table 1.1: Intelligence vs Information and Knowledge	
Intelligence	*Information and Knowledge*
Piques curiosity	Describes, instructs, tells, and prescribes
Engages individual thought process	Is highly defined
Demands comparison and verification	Does not ask for participation or proof
Heightens perceptions	Reflects a completed thought
Is part of a bigger picture (i.e. is inclusive)	Is singular, specialized (exclusive)
Raises a red flag	Warns directly
Has a limited shelf life	Has an infinite duration or historical sequence

People today are more informed than ever. Specialists such as medical and legal professionals, along with consultants, architects and builders, etc. are finding it harder and harder to please clients who have access to vast amounts of previously unattainable information. An employee with any degree of interest will consciously or subconsciously be gathering information that will be of benefit to the company. It is this unique and inexpensive information, brought forward that makes the company knowledge base distinct from the competition. Accessing this information and using the company knowledge base to the fullest will provide foreknowledge of industry trends, developments and events and so secure the competitive edge.

Lateral, big picture-thinking employees, aware of the importance of their individual contribution, will enhance the ability of management to make informed business decisions, understand current market requirements and provide original, relevant products and services.

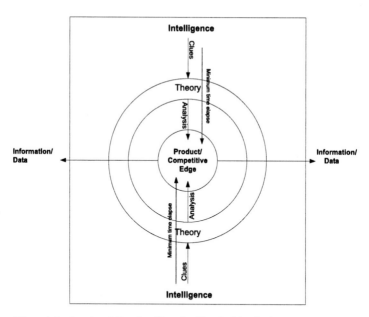

Figure 1.1: A series of Random/Sought Clues **Subjectively Identified** *lead to a Possible Theory that leads to Intelligence that when* **Objectively Analyzed** *and either Corroborated, Incorporated or Rejected can lead to a* **Potential Advantage.** *When policies are followed, this Intelligence can lead to Information or Data about the Potential Advantage.*

Intelligence/Foreknowledge vs. Information

Business Intelligence is also known as foreknowledge. Existing in the future, it is automatically a concept that at best may be described in terms of a balance of probability – what might happen.

Competitive Advantage exists where intelligence is analyzed in a timely fashion and included in policies and initiatives: foreknowledge successfully acted upon, despite the risk factor, in time! (See Figure 1.1)

Competitive Advantage Demystified

Once Intelligence, or its desirability, becomes common knowledge in any given arena, at any point in the process, it becomes information or data; it is in this way that the edge over the competition is lost!

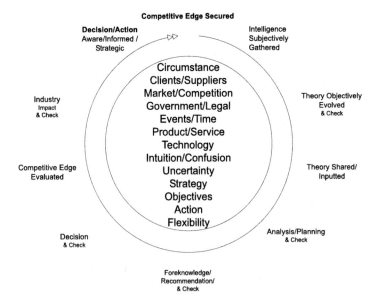

Figure 1.2: The Dynamic Intelligence Continuum (Recommended)

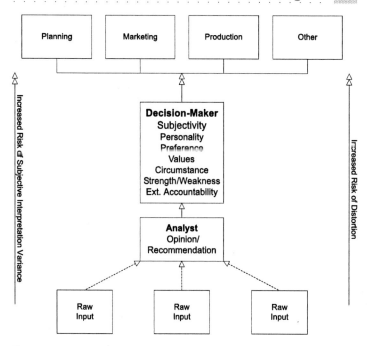

Figure 1.3: A Rigid/Static Intelligence Hierarchy (Not Recommended)

Intelligence and Strategy

Strategy is defined as a plan of action in business or politics and is used in conjunction with words like blueprint, procedure, approach, design, tactic or master-plan. Originally a predominantly militaristic term, it described the best possible tactics to out manoeuvre an enemy on the battle field. These are commonly used terms, but to what extent does *strategy* and *being strategic* impact everyday individual awareness?

Strategy relates to an external *target* group, immediately bringing forward the concept/notion of *competition* or *winning*. Logically, knowledge of external parties and **all** the details/circumstance surrounding their operation would be crucial in a plan or strategy that is designed to be competitive. This knowledge includes tangible and intangible, overt and covert knowledge of target activity at any point in time.

External parties would, from a business viewpoint, refer to clients, suppliers, industry partners, government and of course competitors. Strategy would refer to the plan a given organization/individual has worked out, at any point in time, to effectively align organizational objectives with a *target* interaction.

If any given strategy is a clear component of competition, then intelligence or foreknowledge has to be an integral part of that strategy. Without the ability to forecast events, trends and predict probable outcomes, strategy cannot exist. With leadership and proactive objective setting and decision making, successful strategy and targeted action will remain dynamic and relevant to changing intelligence realities.

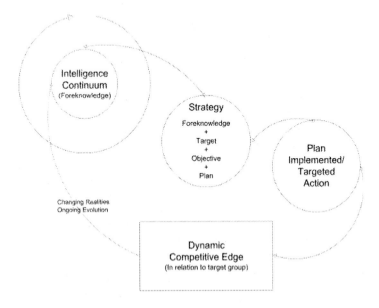

Figure 1.4: The role of intelligence strategy in the intelligence continuum.

Intelligence & Areas of Business Relevance: Who is responsible?

Ultimate responsibility for organizational intelligence policy or culture lies with top management, with the function delegated to Chief Information Officers and systems/technology and, in recent years, Security Department heads. While specific responsibility for gathering intelligence and protecting assets should lie with **every** member of the organization, there are additional operational areas that are crucial to efficient deliverables in this area. These include:

- **Planning, Strategy & Development.** These departments are the obvious first choice. A company would be unable plan and strategize for a competitive future without current intelligence. Planners, strategists and developers ideally are able to gather, process, and analyze intelligence, and translate the result into effective policy recommendations.

- **IT (Information Technology).** Increasingly, this team collectively manages the technical aspects of the internal and external flow of information into and from the company. The modern day vulnerability of classified information, intellectual property, and business secrets is not to be taken lightly. Internet research and the use of competitive intelligence, database, and CRM software (important tools in the processing of intelligence) would fall under this area of expertise and supervision.

- **Sales & Marketing.** Sales and marketing people have the capacity to be the eyes and ears of the company. Gregarious and outgoing, they have widespread industry contact and are able to assess changes in client, supplier, or competitor activity. Recognition of this role has the distinct advantage of creating loyalty and a real sense of belonging in the individual, thus enhancing corporate depth.

- **Media Liaison/Communications.** This team acts as the mouthpiece of the organization and bears the responsibility of ensuring intelligence free information reaches the media and clients. Inquiries from the public, media, and clients will be rich in intelligence; trends, patterns and unusual external interactions should be reported to the responsible members of staff.

- **Field Representatives/Service Personnel.** Agents in the field carry enormous responsibility in representing the corporate image. On the cutting edge, they are uniquely positioned to gather intelligence and report back to head office. Conversely, an unaware, free-talking individual will be a sitting target for any external intelligence seeking initiatives.

- **Human Resources.** A good HR department is the thermostat of any organization. Monitoring symptoms of organizational fatigue, employee discontent, attrition rates, etc. would provide good internal intelligence that would enable timely action. Hiring the appropriate *intelligence profile* would be a crucial function of the department.

The Business Plan & Corporate Intelligence

The Intelligence Cluster

In the corporate/organizational environment, top management, department heads, and selected individuals responsible for planning, strategy, policy, production and development areas, etc. will ideally meet regularly to decide on intelligence priorities. These decisions would then become a flexible part of the corporate operational requirement that will be included in the short or long term business plan.

The Business Plan

The business plan is just that…a plan or wish list . At best, it is a projection or guess as to how the business will evolve – it deals with the future and is therefore *not* reality! The development of a relevant and dynamic business plan will always factor in required intelligence, including random, unknown developments as well as the prospect of what might happen on global, national, industry, and corporate levels. An evolving plan will give advance warning that that the world is unfolding differently; it will provide a yardstick for reality, marrying everyday details with the bigger picture.

Selected departments, teams or individuals who would play key roles in this regard should be identified. Requirements are unpacked at the relevant levels throughout the organization, clearly laying down guidelines in the form of priorities, collection areas and identified targets that will satisfy corporate or organizational requirements.

It is important to keep in mind that:

- Intelligence may be gathered by anyone in the company. The business plan should reflect a knowledge culture that allows intelligence from any source to be brought forward and processed.

- Intelligence priorities and key performance areas should not eclipse nor be confused with the broader intelligence gathering capacity of the intelligence team.

- Performance evaluation should be reflected in the business plan in the form of Key Performance Areas and in turn unpacked into Critical Performance Indicators that will be agreed to with relevant teams and individuals.

- The business plan should allow for a reward system that will acknowledge the importance of individual contribution.

- Timely recognition of change and new developments is vital to organizational relevance and survival. Any business plan must be adapted to changing circumstances. Organizations that cling to targets and objectives rooted in yesterday's criteria will negatively impair the competitive advantage and will put the corporate future at risk.

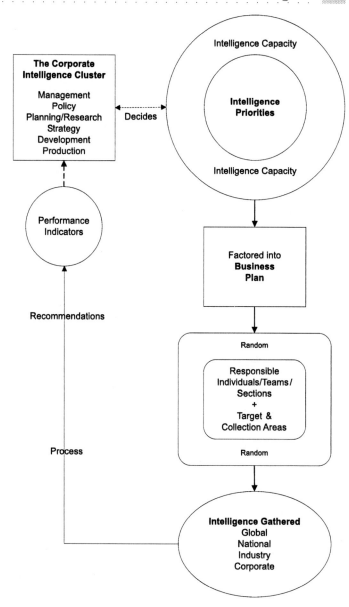

Figure 1.5: The role of the business plan in the intelligence gathering process.

Intelligence Awareness & the *Expert* Role of the Individual

Subjective Gathering of Clues/Heeding *Red flags*

Noticing what is going on around one is part of everyday life. Without knowing it we are endlessly forming and reforming opinions about people and circumstances. Many times, the conscious part of the process is shut down by people who do not want to be considered *judgmental;* this is as ridiculous a notion as excising one of the senses. Noticing detail and formulating opinion is normal. Keeping an open and flexible mind to adjust opinion/judgment is a skill that needs to be practiced!

Change in behaviour, altered appearance, new habits, spending patterns, associations, etc. will all be noticed as something different from the normal or usual pattern – a discordant note or *red warning flag*. Individual members of any organization should be encouraged to become more aware of the importance of their contribution in this regard. It would not be an exaggeration to expect a neighbor to notice untoward or different behavior; hopefully, their observations might save lives or ensure timely protection of property. Would we not be irked in time of emergency by a neighbor who said they preferred not to notice other peoples business?

This is a subjective process and depends entirely on individual experience, learning and interest. The individual role of noticing events, behaviour and developments related to the operation of any given organization will rarely appear on a job description, yet this vital function, known at this stage as gathering raw intelligence, may be what leads to a policy or decision that potentially will improve the rate of success, prevent financial collapse, and save jobs.

Objective Formation/Delivery of Theory

Ideally, once a succession or pattern of clues becomes apparent, the individual will objectively evaluate the possibility of a theory that will be of interest to his or her organization. This means that subjective reaction to stimulus has to be put into an objective perspective to ensure third-party relevance. This exercise usually requires a good deal of thinking and will call on the analytical ability of the individual to cross-reference the new intelligence with knowledge of organizational or industry actualities.

Corroboration will not always be available. Regardless of accuracy, raw intelligence theories should be presented to the relevant organizational channel or (at very least) should be shared with a trusted colleague. True service orientation will ensure that the individual is not daunted by fear of rejection or ridicule when convinced his or her intelligence needs to be shared and considered at a higher level.

Intelligence awareness allows individuals to use valuable expertise they don't know they have. The progression of individual raw intelligence input from colleague to supervisor to organizational well-being to industry relevance to national interest does not require a great stretch of the imagination.

The Enormity of the Individual Contribution

At any point in time, the individual team/organization member will be exposed consciously or sub-consciously to an endless stream of seemingly unrelated information and data. It is the ability to consciously relate potentially interesting or relevant material to a specific job, organization or industry that constitutes Intelligence Awareness.

Sharing intelligence at any level will potentially have a positive impact on organizational relevance, efficiency and profitability. It is suggested that awareness of this role will not only increase a sense of professional worth and belonging, but also will enhance the emotional and social depth of any organization, manifested by a fully engaged and participatory employee group.

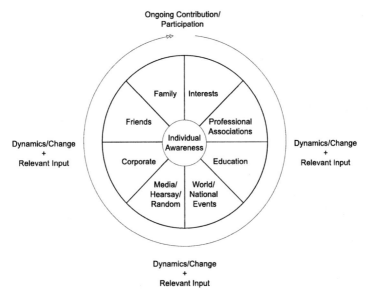

Figure 1.6: The Individual Awareness Continuum.

Individual Intelligence Awareness & Competitive Advantage

While most people in business subconsciously gather intelligence on a daily basis, it is the conscious awareness of what needs to be present for relevant procurement, processing and policy implementation that will result in an intelligence product that that will secure competitive advantage.

The following themes will be repeated continuously throughout the pages of this book.

Acceptance of Uncertainty

Human nature loves the comfort provided by the illusion of certainty. What in life can be predicted with absolute certainty? The harsh reality is that only death at some future point is certain. Intelligence will always be uncertain – accepting that the ever present *wildcard* factor might strike at any moment will be the first step in consciously becoming a good intelligence gatherer, processor and policy maker. Risk, as we know it in business, means nothing more than proceeding with a certain course of action without knowing the exact outcome. Foolish or precipitous action is not recommended, but acting on best case scenarios or a balance of probabilities will bring clear rewards. Decisions made only within known parameters will lead to a conservative and mediocre service or product delivery. On a practical workplace level, fear of being wrong and insistence on quantifiable or absolute proof before new material will be considered are the single biggest factors that stifle creative and innovative input.

The Passage of Time

Never was the cliché *"time waits for no-one"* more appropriate. Once the first clues are noted and a theory is evolved, care must be taken to introduce the raw intelligence into the system as soon as possible. Speed of processing by analysts, developers and planners is equally essential as is their quick recommendation to decision makers. It goes without saying that a quick roll out of policy, product or service will complete all the steps to secure advantage over competitors. Any delay will allow others to potentially discover the same intelligence. As is evident, risk of compromise to the security/secrecy of the intelligence is increased proportionately to the elapse of time from gathering to policy implementation.

Proactive Decision-Making & Leadership

All aspects of the intelligence cycle demand a conscious individual desire to accept responsibility for a bigger picture scenario. This is so because intelligence gathering is usually a role, rather than a duty that is assumed by the individual. Seldom on junior levels will anyone know if available intelligence has been ignored. Fundamental to effective decision-making is a preparedness to work boldly with evolving circumstance, time, uncertainty and risk in the context of a specific organization and its product or service. Flexibility in setting objectives that reflect changing business scenarios is essential.

A true leader understands that a strong service orientation gives real meaning to the risk involved in exploring vision, creativity and innovation.

Intelligence Awareness ... An Ongoing State of Mind

It does not require a stretch of the imagination to believe that most members of an organization are more productive if they feel needed, appreciated and have some sense of belonging to a workplace community. An occasional after-hours event or social outing does not achieve this goal. Consider: if people are happiest when they are using *all* innate and learned ability then it is logical that an organization would benefit if it ensures that each individual is

- Aware of his or her ability,

- Uses that ability to the fullest, and

- Is recognized for individual contribution.

The resulting well being will inspire the desire to perpetuate the current circumstance and conditions to further his or her career path in a particular organization. Anything that threatens this state of being will be strongly opposed.

We are talking about loyalty!

All individuals should be encouraged to discuss any industry, product developments and perceived threats or unusual behavior that might be relevant to the organization's well being. The investment in this type of exercise will create an added sense of personal worth as will recognition for a job well done.

- Show genuine interest

- Take care not to dismiss colleagues/employees who present half-developed theories and disjointed information

- Ask questions to get more detail (who/when/where/circumstances)

- Express thanks

- Input the information into the system

This is an inexpensive and efficient way to stay current, and enhance a sense of corporate depth.

Recognizing and utilizing individual worth is the greatest acknowledgement that an employee can receive. Loyalty is arguably the most valuable corporate commodity in time of crisis.

Interconnectivity & the Business Intelligence Arena

In the immediate, intelligence will focus around a specific, product, industry, company or individual. The bigger picture encompasses a much greater playing field. The ripple effect of an event or development in any **Global, National, Industry** or **Corporate** area may have far reaching effects. Timely intelligence of any such event and its potential impact will provide the opportunity to secure the competitive edge.

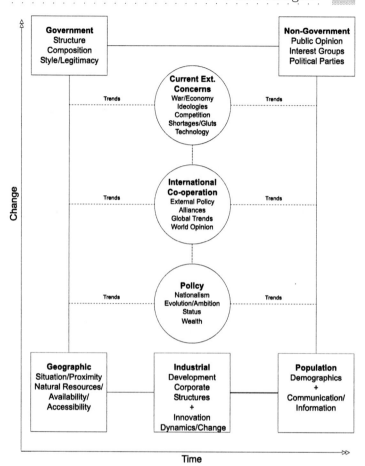

Figure 1.7

The Intelligence Objective

Specific Intelligence Objectives

Any company, in the course of identifying operational requirements and tasks necessary to achieve defined goals will look at what is already known and identifiable as well as what might not be readily apparent. The latter is what would constitute the intelligence objective. This requirement is broken down into precise tasks and the collection process begins. It will always be crucial that a company discover targeted information about an industry, competitor, or client as well as international, regional, political, and economic specifics. Objectives will be set and directives given in order to procure as much information as possible within given people, resources, funding, and time parameters. The exercise will be run pretty much along the lines of any project that the company would undertake in the course of its operation. Objectives of this nature would focus on a competitor's product, client-base, profits margins, government subsidies, etc.

Intelligence Gathering - The Bigger Picture

There is no way to be on top of intelligence problems unless you collect much more extensively than any cost accounting approach would justify, and then rely on the wisdom and experience of analysts to sift out the small percentage of vital information that needs to be passed on to the top of government ...

US comment on lessons learned from the British approach to intelligence gathering in WWII. (*Alan Turing: The Enigma*, Andrew Hodges)

Hidden/Unspecified Intelligence Objectives

We are surrounded by knowledge that we do not realize exists. The idea is to create an awareness that will allow the investigation of random observations and thoughts that may give rise to a theory that would become a potential source of intelligence.

Interaction is unavoidable. We talk to others, listen and are subject to a daily barrage of detail, facts and information that, for the most part, becomes part of the subconscious memory. A chance word, event or comment might trigger a memory and even send up a red flag. Depending on the intensity and frequency of this experience, this stored information will be accessed. The importance of the subject matter might demand the creation of a more conscious/available record for easy reference.

It is intelligence gathering of this nature that is the most difficult to secure as there are no defined objectives and points of predictable reference. The natural

---

Ungraspability?

The terms *stopping* and *seeing* basically cannot be separated. They mean concentration and insight. When thoughts arise, you should investigate the thought: Where is it? Where does it come from? Where does it disappear? Push this inquiry on and on … then you will see where the thought arises. You don't need to seek the point of arising anymore … Once you reach this *ungraspability*, then as before you continuously practice stopping and continue it by seeing…Listening means listening to the soundless; looking means looking at the formless…

"The Secret of the Chinese Flower", *The Classic Chinese Book of Life*

tendency to insist on certainty becomes a huge obstacle at this point in the intelligence process - Being on the lookout for something that is not defined is a difficult concept for many to understand.

Covert Intelligence Objectives

Given that 90% of intelligence gathering is overt in nature and overwhelmingly abundant and obtainable to everyone, it is easy to overlook the remaining 10% of intelligence that requires covert gathering, unless absolutely necessary. The current economic, social and political structure of the world as we know it has shrunk to the extent that a corporation's future success or competitive edge will possibly be decided in this small realm.

DISCRETION VS SECRECY

Good intelligence is something akin to a good poker hand. It needs to be recognized, analyzed, and utilized. Prematurely showing other players your hand would blow any advantage away. The search for intelligence, the target, the process and the players (collector and source) need to be kept as discreet as possible as an awareness of these factors would in turn become intelligence for competitors. We live in a corporate environment where most of the players know the rules of the game. The winners will have the best strategies and the most stamina.

Clandestine operations by their very nature tend to attract attention, especially in today's world where information and technology sharing are unavoidable. An aware, thinking individual will be able to proceed along an unknown path confident of the ability to manage whatever presents itself along the way.

Acceptance that the intelligence collection process can only be managed and not controlled is a vital key to a successful intelligence operation.

Heisenberg Uncertainty Principle

It is impossible to know simultaneously both momentum (mass x velocity) and the position of a particle; therefore, it follows that we cannot talk about electrons circling the nucleus in well-defined orbits.

What then is certain? All particles move all the time.

Intelligence & the Value of Awareness - Practical Scenarios

Scenario 1 (Short term, immediate impact)

Company:

IT World Learning(ITWL), incorporated in Canada (fictitious)

Mission:

Recruit IT students, from Asia, notably India and China

Fact:

75% of students derived from recruiting drives in India

Clues:

1. October 2001 - CEO of large Industrial Empire berates ITWL CFO at a reception for allowing Canada's technical *know how* to leave the country... Rants about hiring cheap coding expertise in India - "Untaxed salary," "Work without a permit," etc.

2. October 2001 - Small newspaper article reporting the trend of Indian businessmen buying defunct North American IT companies + rights to software.

3. November 2001 - Friend at electronics company reports overwork. Indian nationals on temporary visa permits have been *let go*.

4. December 2001 - Draft anti-terror legislation includes cryptic phrase: "Prevent outflow of technology."

Intelligence (not certain, not common knowledge): ·

There is an unexplained attitude shift on business and government levels regarding the preservation of national intellectual property and technology advantage, specifically regarding India.

Intelligence Theory:

- The immigration act may be amended curtailing capacity to recruit abroad.

- An increased sensitivity/awareness regarding the protection of Canadian strategic technology may lead to governmental action.

Window of opportunity provided by Intelligence - Action Options:

- Do nothing and risk losing 75% of business overnight.

- Rapidly implement a marketing drive internally and ascertain which countries abroad could be appropriate alternate markets. (No Risk!)

- Investigate the big picture consequences and strategize to secure a possible advantage.

February 2002:

- Changes made to the Immigration Act: Limitations on granting of student visas.

- *Competitive Intelligence Advantage lost.*

- *Intelligence has become information.*

May 2003: (Re-emergence of Intelligence theory as open/ general opinion or cause for concern.)

Editorial in *Toronto Star* May 5th 2003 entitled "Keep Technology in Canadian Hands."

The piece calls on the Canadian government to reject the Commons Industry, Science & Technology Committee recommendation to lift restrictions and do away with requirements currently in place to ensure majority Canadian ownership and control of information and communications technology organizations.

The editorial underscores the strategic importance of maintaining control of this key sector of the economy and warns against the erosion of Canada's position of influence as a world leader in the industry.

It is important to note that, for Canadians, the editorial is not intelligence but information. The information is that the Canadian telecommunications industry is warned that it is at risk. Similarly all debates in this regard would be information. Peripheral intelligence might, however, be gleaned from following any arguments that support or oppose this standpoint.

The article, however, would be of possible intelligence value for an external country/organization interested in securing ownership of Canadian technology.

Interesting Observations:

- The scope of the issue is broader than previously thought ; it is not limited to Indian encroachment. The Committee recommendations will result in government decision making that will affect the existence or lack of intelligence

- A window of strategic opportunity existed for a period of nearly 18 months from when the first intelligence clue appeared for an interested bid to gain control of desired Canadian technology. A similar period existed for the government, organizations and individuals to allow/prevent the sale/outflow of Canadian technology.

- The Committee's argument for lifting ownership restrictions is couched in terms of encouraging investment that would reduce capital expenditure. A degree of disciplined thought is required to avoid seduction by short-term gain.

- All action taken in this regard will be subject to media attention, with the possibility of a national debate.

- *Competitive Intelligence Advantage lost.*

- *Intelligence has become information.*

Scenario 2 (Medium term, gradual impact)

Company:

AeroAmerica, South American aircraft builder (fictitious)

Mission:

Supplies jet aircraft worldwide in a highly competitive market.

Fact:

Since 1995 China has become an increasingly important client; because of local expansion and projected growth, it is considered a *safe* business area.

Clues:

1. July 1999 - China overhauls its aviation industry structure into large and small aircraft industry, plus suppliers of parts to major North American players (AVIC I& II).

2. January 2002 - Competitors appear to be jittery and concentrating on the Chinese Market more than usual.

3. February 2002 - The requests by Chinese clients for tours of the factory have noticeably increased.

4. March 2002 - It has been noticed that foreign Aviation experts have been invited to China with greater frequency and report unusually lavish treatment.

5. There are reported rumors of a *state-of-the-art* Chinese aeronautics design team.

6. April 2002 - Civil Aviation Administration of China reports a need for 1500 new passenger jets by 2020; yet, this is not at all reflected in discussions with clients.

Intelligence (not certain, not common knowledge): ·

The behavior of Chinese aviation clients, company competitors and the existing supplier/purchaser relationship reflect a changed shift in emphasis from product to manufacture.

Intelligence Theory + Objectives:

- China may be poised to become a player in the jet aircraft supply business.

- This will have a negative impact on expected future business with China and will potentially erode company/national position in an already competitive market.

- The new company may be a potential purchaser of strategic equipment.

- Objective: discover Chinese aviation industry realities.

Window of opportunity provided by Intelligence - Action Options:

- Urgently ascertain future requirements of secret AVIC I & II aircraft production.

- Urgently secure preferred supplier/strategic alliance status with AVIC I & II.

- Explore, as a priority, new client possibilities.

October 2002:

- AVIC launches commercial venture "to supply advanced regional jets for the 21st century" and has invited tenders for developing engines and electronic systems.

- *Competitive Intelligence Advantage lost.*

- *Intelligence has become information.*

Scenario 3 (Long term, immediate impact)

Company:

West Coast Timber, British Columbia Canada (fictitious)

Mission:

Canadian timber exporters

Fact:

U.S. Imports 60% of product

Clues:

- July 1997 - Grumbling from US timber producers at low cost of Canadian wood

- 1998 - Continued complaints from producers

- 1999-2000 - Increasing signs that the issue is has become an internal political issue in the US

- 2000-2001 - Widespread calls in US for governmental action

Intelligence (not common knowledge):

Canadian companies should realize that the US timber market is facing imminent change and is in jeopardy.

Intelligence Theory: ·

US government action can be expected to either place a levy on and/or curtail Canadian timber imports. There may be company and/or national consequences.

Window of opportunity provided by Intelligence - Action Options:

- Urge the Canadian authorities to lobby their counterparts, using all available leverage to prevent US government interference.

- Strategize to lay down a punitive and effective response.

- Engage in media drama to draw world attention to the issue.

- Urgently seek alternate markets.

- Plan/budget for industry/company cutbacks and layoffs.

August 2001: ·

- The United States slaps a 19.3% preliminary penalty tariff on lumber imported from Canada.

- *Competitive Intelligence Advantage lost.*

- *Intelligence has become information.*

Scenario 4 (Short term, unknown impact)

Company:

None

Mission:

None

Fact:

Your spouse works for a small company (head office is in Regina, Saskatchewan) that is involved in research of human genetics and bioinformatics. There is only one other such company in Canada, situated in St. John's, Newfoundland.

Clues:

At the Toronto airport, a conversation takes place with an individual connecting with a Europe bound flight. From an earlier cell-phone conversation it has been detected that he is

- Not from North America (possibly Swedish)

- Is involved with a company buy out

- Is under pressure from his office

- His *BlackBerry* cover/case has a **BioMatica** logo (name changed for this example)

He complains that for a country involved in high-tech industry and research, he cannot understand why the airport at St. John's cannot seem to enter his air mile points accurately. He adds that he has made a least six such trips in the last few months and every time there has been a problem. He asks if it would perhaps be better in Regina as he will probably be visiting there soon.

When asked if he is in the biotech industry, he clams up. There is no further discussion.

Intelligence (not common knowledge):

A European company is potentially buying out a unique Canadian operation and has its eye on another. The individual at the airport is hiding something.

Intelligence Theory: ·

Is BioMatica looking to corner the global market? There may be national and/or personal consequences.

Window of opportunity provided by Intelligence - Action Options:

- Do nothing (High risk)

- Engage and sell your spouse on the urgent need for action if this is a worst case scenario (job security, national interest, etc.) (No risk)

- Lobby national interest groups (No risk)

Today: ·

- BioMatica announces the takeover of the Regina and St. John's companies.

- *Competitive Intelligence Advantage lost.*

- *Intelligence has become information.*

Scenario 5 (Long term, unknown impact)

Company:

ABC Microchip Inc. (Fictitious)

Mission:

Provide micro chips to the computer and cell phone industries

Fact:

Micro chips are made from Coltan which is mined exclusively in Democratic Republic of the Congo.

Clues:

October 2002 - Radio interview on CBC about saving the gorillas of the Congo decries the threat of Coltan mining on the endangered species.

August 5-7, 2002 - The Centre National d'Appui au Développement et à la Participation Populaire (CENADEP) and Partnership Africa Canada (PAC), organised a workshop titled *"Diamonds and the Plunder of the Democratic Republic of Congo's Natural Resources."* Inter alia the conference decided to

- Disseminate information on fraudulent practices in the mining sector, especially with diamonds and Coltan, aimed at appropriate national and international controls.

- Promote public awareness of the D.R.C.'s numerous natural resources through press conferences, press releases, radio and television programmes and other publications and exert pressure on transit/trading countries to prevent plunder.

November 2002: Environmental Science & Technology warns of microchip price hikes estimating that it takes at least 1.6 kilograms of fossil fuels and chemical inputs to produce a single two-gram memory chip for personal computers.

Intelligence (not common knowledge): ·

Coltan is a virtually unknown commodity; its relevance to the industry is not widely recognized. Movements to curtail the limited Coltan mining resources are intensifying their actions and campaigns.

Intelligence Theory: ·

The availability of Coltan may be at risk. Potential controls could result in drastic price increases with a ripple effect throughout the electronic, computer and cell-phone industries.

Window of opportunity provided by Intelligence - Action Options:

- Stockpile as much Coltan as possible.

- Set research in motion for an alternate supply or replacement material.

- Lobby the national government to negotiate Coltan purchase agreements with the DRC as soon as possible.

Competitive Intelligence Advantage Pending ·

- The connection of Coltan with the microchip industry in the general public opinion and the consequent rise in price will remove any existing competitive advantage.

- There is a high risk of competition from US and European manufacturers.

Scenario Comment & Interpretation

The first three scenarios are based on real-life intelligence situations derived from media reports. It is clear from looking at each step that the intelligence process is not complicated and largely common sense.

The success of the different scenarios, or rather the successful use of intelligence in all four cases hinges on an **awareness** of:

- The *chance* factor in intelligence gathering

- A particular industry/company (general or specific) knowledge

- How that industry impacts on personal and national well being

- People and their behavior

- How individual behavior translates into useful information about a specific industry

- Repeated information prompts a recall of previous information or clues

- The large degree that unrelated events connect

- How a series of clues gives rise to an intelligence theory

- The need for a theory to be shared with/sold to others (even if uncertain or ultimately incorrect) if any advantage is to be had

- The consideration of action options

- The importance of deciding to take action

- The importance of individual action in the larger community's survival and well being

- The temporary shelf life of intelligence

- The fact that once intelligence becomes certain and common knowledge, competitive advantage is lost

Following these observations, the required competencies for corporate or organizational awareness would be:

- The conscious desire to stay informed and aware.

- Creative, lateral and strategic thinking, able to see isolated events in terms of the bigger picture.

- The ability to understand and interpret people and situations.

- A logical decision-making process that responds rather than reacts to external stimuli.

- A strong service or leadership orientation.

- Oral and written communication competence, with the ability to sell uncertain, unproven and abstract concepts.

- The willingness to accept failure and rejection as normal aspects of business life.

Awareness is the key!

Personal Intelligence Awareness Check!

Demystifying Innate Intelligence Gathering Ability - Using Common Sense and Accessing Relationships

When considering the purchase of a car, computer or property, etc., what procedure do you follow?

Would you buy the first item you saw?

Would you consider previous experience?

Would you research the subject?

How would you conduct the research?

Would you consult an expert/authority?

Would you call on friends or family for advice?

How quickly do you usually come to a decision?

What level of confidence do you normally have in your decisions?

Do you ever change your decision?

How does this make you feel?

Do you remain alert to the possibility of new product development, price increase/cuts, availability etc.?

How do you do this?

How often do your contacts volunteer information once they know your requirements?

Have you ever made bad decisions/purchases?

To what extent were these decisions based on outside influence?

Did you go with *gut*?

In making your decision, did you consider long term consequence?

Did you factor in the end user(s)?

What do you do when a bad purchase has become apparent?

To what extent do you share your findings with others?

Are you prepared to offer information without being asked?

Are you often asked for advice when people make purchases?

To what extent do you maintain an ongoing awareness of the subject/product once a purchase has been made?

Would you agree that intelligence gathering is part of your everyday life?

Secondary Intelligence

The analysis or distillation of readily available information or data by a specific organization or individual can in itself produce new intelligence.

Bearing in mind that intelligence is a series of clues that gives rise to a potentially relevant and useful theory, analysis of information or data by an aware and creative mind will in turn give rise to more clues and more theories. The process of analysis (random or focused) will become the potential realm of raw intelligence.

Actual intelligence discovered may be in the form of industry trends, client spending patterns, etc. or general socioeconomic or political predictions that might or might not affect a specific business or industry.

When new technologies impose themselves on societies long habituated to older technologies, anxieties of all kinds result. Our electronic world now calls for a unified field of global awareness; the kind of private consciousness appropriate to literate man can be viewed as an unbearable kink in the collective consciousness demanded by electronic information movement. In this impasse, suspension of all automatic reflexes would seem to be in order. I believe that artists, in all media, respond soonest to the challenges of new pressures. I would like to suggest that they also show us ways of living with new technology without destroying earlier forms and achievements. The new media, too, are not toys; they should not be in the hands of Mother Goose and Peter Pan executives. They can be entrusted only to new artists.

Marshall McLuhan

Awareness & Efficient Distillation of Secondary Intelligence

- The thinking of others should be corroborated wherever possible. This is easier said than done. We usually tend to consider the written word as valid. Internet searches are especially tricky in this regard – a recognizable format and good layout have great persuasive value. Past positive corroboration should not lull the intelligence gatherer into a false sense of security or confidence.

- All intelligence should be factored into the context of organizational, product or service individuality. The temptation to recycle the analysis of outsiders as the first option is always present.

- The intelligence search (goals and activity) will always potentially signal personal and organizational objectives to the outside. New privacy legislation, computer firewalls and the like will not easily counter the intensity of the profiling activity that pervades our society today. Even the internet *spy catchers* are profiling their clients!

- *Most probable* as opposed to *certain* will be the best description of the results obtained. Acceptance of this status will ensure flexibility and the ongoing search for fresh intelligence.

Intelligence & Technology

Advances in technology have blessed the intelligence world with an incredible array of tools to assist in the procurement and processing of information. Today, when one hears terminology such as *Competitive Intelligence, Client Relationship Management, Knowledge Management, Presentation Skills, etc.* tracking software, data base applications, computer profiling, PowerPoint™ and other technical applications are often what spring to mind. Tools and processes are becoming synonymous with human service.

Reliance solely on technology in intelligence collection has three distinct dangers:

- Technology and information/data that is generally available will at best provide an illusion of advantage as they are also available to competitors and the general public.

- Preoccupation with known processes and predictable information gathering will potentially inhibit innovation and original thinking.

- Data becomes stale the moment it is mined – a failure to renew intelligence might produce inaccurate information that will be a considerable cost to the company on administrative, planning and strategic levels.

Important Guidelines in the use of Business Intelligence Technology

- Regard technology as a tool or extension of human analytical competency. Never underestimate the value of human interpretation

- In the event of purchasing business intelligence products, understand that the same product might be sold to your competitor – you will be effectively feeding at the same trough! The known fact that your organization uses a certain technology will in itself be an item of intelligence for interested outsiders.

- Be alert for the *wild card* factor – it is ever present!

The Human mind remains the strongest factor in the intelligence gathering process because, as opposed to programmed technology, it is capable of generating original thought and the ability to deal with new and unpredictable situations as they unfold. The tendency of the intelligence world to increasingly rely on technology is reflected by governments and corporations in most of the developed world. A current illustration of this trend would be the example set by the US government. In the last decade the NSA spent approximately $28 billion per annum on sophisticated information gathering procedures: satellite surveillance and monitoring/ eavesdropping facilities such as that at Menwith Hill, Yorkshire in the UK, gathered and stored tons of raw information. In contrast, only $2 billion per annum was allocated to process this information. (The latter figure represented the entire budget allocation of the CIA at that time.)

Technology cannot do more than process, within a known context, what is already recorded. Can technology replace the natural curiosity of the human mind?

Can Machines Think?

With the vast array of proven technology at the service of the industrialized regions of the world, it is has long been foolish to argue that (for the most part) humans can out-perform machines. For nearly a century it has been clear that inter alia, human physical performance is no match for an aircraft, automobile or most modern industrial equipment.

The steady evolution of the computer era over the last half-century has further underscored the extent of this phenomenon. Canada's Marshall McLuhan (he coined the terms *Global Village* and "The Medium is the Message") warned more than thirty years ago that technology should be seen as the *extension rather than a replacement of human capacity*. In other words, technology and machines are tools that can give greater expression to human genius and creativity. Performance should not be confused with thinking, speed with intelligence. Intelligence refers to the innate human capacity to think creatively when faced with the unknown or unproven.

The Turing Test for Intelligence

Increasingly, Information Technology has provided systems that can file, archive, search, retrieve, cross-reference and interconnect within seconds. On cue, huge amounts of data are available with a speed that cannot be matched by the human brain. Is it not possible then that we can be forgiven for thinking that a computer can think? The challenge is not new: in the early 1950s, Alan Turing, the unsung hero of WWII whose brilliance spearheaded the decoding of the Nazi ENIGMA encryption system, saving thousands of lives, pondered this very question.

Turing predicted that computers would evolve to a point where they would be programmed to mimic human intelligence. His simple test would involve the interrogation of a machine and a human with answers provided textually (a teleprinter at the time):

> "It is proposed that a machine may be deemed intelligent, if it can act in such a manner that a human cannot distinguish the machine from another human merely by asking questions via a mechanical link.

> "We are then, testing the machine's intelligence via the computer's ability to fool **our** intelligence within a particular context. Put yet another way, if **we** are not intelligent enough to solve the riddle, then we will call the machine intelligent (like us?)."
> (Alan Turing)

Debate for and against the notion that a computer could replace or rival human thinking has continued ever since. Providers of modern day *thinking* computers promise that their products will secure competitive advantage, cost/time efficiency and increased profits. Has technology advanced to this level of sophistication? Can we rely on computer systems to perform crucial functions in the role of final authority?

It might well be inferred that a company or individual that considers the equations in Table 1.2 (previous) to be exclusively true has tacitly admitted that computers can replace human thinking.

Table 1.2: Common thinking that indicates an underlying belief that computers can replace humans		
Client Relationship Management (CRM)	=	IT/Database/Tracking software
Competitive Intelligence (CI)	=	IT/Database/Information cross-referencing
Customer Service	=	Template-driven call centre
Career Development	=	Computer-driven profiling/prediction

Alan Turing believed in the evolution of computers and their ultimate competence yet did not dismiss the traditional arguments against the premise that machines can think. They ranged from proven mathematical uncertainty to the myriad differences gender, culture, life experience and language bring to the thinking and communication (expression of thinking) process. Today, these factors still bring uncertainty to those who would like to believe a machine is able to provide an unequivocal result and complete accuracy.

Fifty years after the Turing Test came into being it is interesting to consider the following:

- People program computers

- People request, access and process computer data

- People service/upgrade computers

- People provide energy that drives computers

- People are still faced with the unknown

- People are imperfect and therefore fallible....

Has technology reached the point where it can override human irrationality and fallibility?

Has technology reached the point where it can transcend language, cultural and experiential differences/ interpretation?

Can a computer calculate or predict outcomes of unknown scenarios?

Can a computer deal with abstract, intangible or unrecorded concepts?

Can a computer imagine or generate original thought?

Is a computer naturally curious?

Can a computer rival/replace human thinking?

World human chess champion Vladimir Kramnik locked in battle with computer star Deep Fritz, in the *Brains in Bahrain* contest, exposed flaws in the computer's technique. The computer that can evaluate 3.5 million moves per second, according to press reports, could not break the young Russian's defence.

When asked whether Kramnik thought his play was perfect, the world champion responded modestly:

> "One can never play perfect chess, but I think I played quite well today." He added, "If the computer is to win, it has to be through tactics. In this game, the computer could not grasp many of my ideas because they were too abstract." (October 2002)

Corporate Asset Protection

It is a given that your competitor or the media is gathering information about your organization. For this reason, protecting corporate assets is the flip side of intelligence gathering – expertise in one will guarantee awareness in the other. Compartmentalization should be avoided.

Prevent Information Leaks

Every day, people talk about their work. Often, even the most casual listener may become privy to the inner workings of an organization. Although there is no firm way to control this phenomenon, it can be managed by creating an organization-wide awareness of what constitutes corporate assets and what will happen if they are compromised.

Employee awareness, for example, that talking about company cash flow problems will result in potential client loss or damage to investor confidence, which will in turn mean layoffs, should have the effect of bringing a degree of discretion to casual conversation. The extreme privilege our society enjoys has resulted in a sort of naiveté in this respect. Espionage, corporate or otherwise is a cloak and dagger business that happens elsewhere or in movies and novels.

It is important to relate lack of corporate depth and employee loyalty directly to organizational vulnerability to espionage, intentional or inadvertent. The constant downsizing, buyouts/mergers and reorganizations that have characterized the business culture throughout the nineties and into this century, have somewhat undermined employee confidence in the relatively secure corporate climate that was enjoyed since WWII. Similarly the resulting uncertainty of the individual career path has resulted in erosion of basic values such as loyalty and accountability. The product of this culture, the *'whatever'* type employee, is one of the most significant corporate areas of risk.

Unnecessary sharing of information - *Prudence vs Paranoia*

All employees need to be careful about what they disclose. Indiscrete discussion of business deals in public has caused many clients to take their business elsewhere. It should be clear that this does not mean operating in a climate of secrecy and paranoia. Reliance on intuition and gut plays an important part in knowing *who is learning what about the organization.*

A simple rule to follow is: "Why am I saying this and to whom am I saying it?" If no satisfactory answer springs to mind, say nothing! The best reason for talking would be to sell your organization and your own ability when necessary. Clearly it can be seen there is no hard and fast rule – to sell, we need to talk; to be safe, we need to shut up! Walking this tightrope needs skill and (once again) involves navigating the unknown path. Your awareness of asset protection will parallel your ability to recognize intelligence leaks in other organizations.

Broad Asset Protection Guidelines

- Careless talk costs money. Talk with a purpose: say no more than is necessary when talking about work and sensitive issues.

- Be careful when talking about work-related issues.

- Practice speaking in sound bytes: clearly, correctly and concisely.

- If called by a stranger, ask them to identify themselves, and ask where they heard of you/got your name.

- When approached, make others *work* for information . Ask questions such as: "I'd be happy to answer that. Would you like to make an appointment?" or "Why are you asking?"

- Exercise caution when sending electronic messages.

- Obey/follow corporate guidelines when using the Internet: firewalls, anti-virus, cookie settings, encryption of e-mails and hard disk, etc.

- Maintain your computer system/server and keep backup logs.

- Clear your mailbox and store data in a safe database regularly.

- Think before you press *Send.* E-mails are dangerous: be aware that every message can be tracked and recovered.

- Avoid giving friends and family software or database downloads from your server.

- Monitor exposure to business partners, associates and other third parties. Ensure their due diligence to security. Insist upon periodic security audits and vulnerability assessments.

Whether we like it or not competitive intelligence and data mining systems are on the prowl. Try not to make it easy for them. The individual and organizations are open to tracking devices via online surveillance, credit card transactions, consumer watch, license-plate/driving records, criminal records, property registration, social security, medical records, workman compensation, national address list etc.

Safeguard IT Systems, Electronic/Wireless Communication

- How secure is your IT system?

- Is unauthorized access detectable?

- Is your system able to repel intrusion?

- Do you have emergency recovery steps in place to restore systems/information?

- Are you able to fully assess the extent of potential intrusion, track the attacker and repair damage?

- How would you rate your confidence in your process and team in crisis management?

Be aware of the ***daily*** opportunity for a single person to let slip confidential/strategic/secret organizational detail. (See Figure 1.8.)

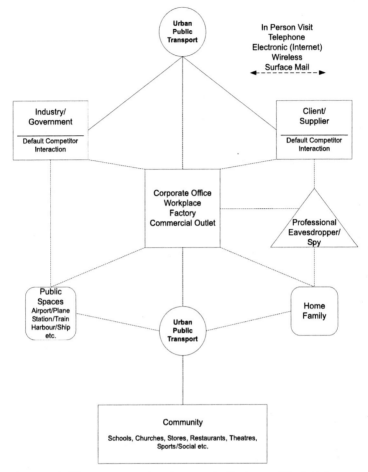

Figure 1.8: There are many places in everyone's life where confidential information may be inadvertently leaked.

Eavesdropping

Inappropriate...or Unavoidable?

A visit to any airport or any intense gathering of people
will bear witness to at least one person engaged in a loud
cell-phone conversation, totally oblivious to all concerned,
spewing forth detail most would prefer not to hear. But
hear it we do! Similarly people talk, work on laptops and
read work related stuff in public.

Is it impolite or unethical to listen in, glance at or
read material that is all but foisted upon us? I, for one,
find that following the drift of these conversations can be
fascinating as well as a valuable source of intelligence.
During a recent trip that involved three air flights (three
departures & three arrivals) I consciously set out to glean
as much business intelligence as possible.

I listened to:

- Two attractive women who alerted the entire
  waiting hall to the fact that they were lawyers
  involved in a complicated and imminent merger
  between two well-known companies. Names and
  personal details of key players were freely bandied
  about

- A *pacing* executive who called his office, wife and
  what appeared to be an assistant/mistress several
  times bossily issuing instructions that divulged his
  name; company name; business; purpose of the
  trip; names and phone numbers of third parties;
  as well as his personal financial situation. The
  latter clearly involved quite a *juggle* if he was to
  make it over the next while!

- Two disgruntled company employees (seemed to be sales types) who discussed their company's prospects - not good at all given the level of financial difficulty disclosed and convoluted company survival strategies that they clearly felt were doomed to failure. The company detail exposed showed an appalling lack of discretion.

I also read:

- A draft letter of resignation of a senior financial person that expressed refusal to be further party to questionable accounting practices...she left her lap top *live* while she went to the washroom!

The interesting thing to remember about this kind of material is that it is, for the most part, delivered by people seemingly oblivious to their surroundings – one sees how easy it is to ostensibly shut out a potential audience. Bistros and cafes that have people cheek on jowl with each other have taught us to simply tune strangers out. That does not mean they have disappeared!

Inadvertent Indiscretion

During one of my diplomatic postings in the eighties, I evolved a good friendship with a colleague from a foreign country. We often visited in each others' homes and shared many interests. He had always presented himself as a career diplomat (Foreign Affairs) – I had no reason to question this fact.

He and his wife had a great book collection from which I was regularly invited to select reading material. One day, taking home a book that approximated an exposé of NATO/Soviet naval activity in the context of the Cold War, I noticed a handwritten note placed inside the cover. It read: "Stefan, I see they got you…." and mentioned an acronym that turned out to be that of a covert naval espionage organization.

In an instant I re-evaluated all I new about Stefan. His passion for the sea, love of ships, a strong interest in communications technology, recent holiday destinations and memorabilia displayed in his home as well as his previous diplomatic postings all began to tell a story. The book only mentioned the possible existence of the organization that monitors super power undersea activity. Three handwritten lines on a piece of scrap paper, a book, available in any bookstore, and my innocent knowledge of a friend proved not only the existence of the organization, but exposed a top secret agent and his sphere of operations. In those days the stakes were high – lives depended on complete secrecy.

In less dramatic circumstances, consider how inadvertent carelessness might betray the business that provides your own livelihood. We live in an age where information sharing is advantageous. This should not blind us to *what people need to know.*

Again, while not advocating a paranoiac approach to security, an awareness of the significance of everything we say and do within the framework of individual, team, corporate, industry and national objectives should become second nature. Good accountable process with creative imagination will go a long way to preventing inadvertent breaches of information security.

- Remember the need-to-know rule! Share information with people only if you have a good reason to do so. This does not mean that you should avoid sharing/brainstorming, but rather a rational decision taken situation by situation, person by person.

- Be aware that a careless slip, insignificant in itself, might provide the missing piece, allowing someone to join the dots in an intelligence sequence.

- Accept that to err is human. The large unknown – the area of business that cannot be nailed down – can be managed only to one's best ability.

- As always, keep an eye out for the inadvertent indiscretion of others!

Outsourcing the Intelligence Role

The notion of hiring an expert to provide a corporate/ organizational service that cannot be provided as well internally due to factors such as time, expertise and resource availability is sound in principle. This would be cause for top-management debate on a scenario by scenario basis.

Caution must be taken though, to ensure that overall responsibility and complementary internal roles are not abandoned in the process. This caveat could not be more true in the case of both intelligence gathering and protection. Intelligence awareness goes to the core and very survival of any organization. Those with the greatest interest will naturally exercise the greatest care in ensuring organizational survival. None has a bigger investment in an organization than a happy and fulfilled employee.

Logically, the moment that an external service provider is engaged to take care of the intelligence aspect of any organization, cause for concern may arise in the fact that

- The number of people aware of specific intelligence objectives is increased.

- The corporate well-being and employee loyalty issues of the service provider, and associated business risks, become inextricably linked with those of the hiring organization.

- Service providers will always be tempted or even requested to download what has worked elsewhere. Management consultancy in all areas of business has to guard against damaging the client's competitive advantage by either consciously or inadvertently sharing solutions elsewhere.

Intelligence Service Outsourcing Guidelines

- Remember that Intelligence awareness and ownership of organizational well-being cannot be outsourced.

- Build an ongoing relationship of trust with any intelligence service provider.

- Insist on exclusivity/confidentiality agreements. Confidentiality should even extend to the fact that the intelligence service has been engaged.

- Outsource specific/limited project requirements only.

- Work on a *need to know* basis. Safeguard bigger picture details from the service provider.

- Monitor service progress on an ongoing basis. Assign permanent contact persons and clear instructions on what constitutes a security breach.

- Awareness, not control, is the key.

Intelligence & External Consultants

Should the services of an outsourced consultant be required to provide a level of intelligence expertise not available internally, ensure that the following checklist is applied. A good intelligence consultant will have the ability to quickly and efficiently:

Assess Your (the Client's) Requirements
Listen, Observe, Ask, Check

Conceptualize a Solution
Create a Vision, Establish Viability

Communicate Requirement/Concept
Transfer Information/Delegate/Instruct/Clarify

Collaboratively Evolve a Solution
Research, Stay Flexible, Ask for Help, Delegate

Sell you (the Client) the Solution
Establish Relevance, Inspire Confidence, Stay Competitive, Remain Flexible, Verify, Rework/Resell

Implement/Manage the Project
Manage People/Resources/Budget/Quality and Time Parameters

Brief End Users

Make the solution/material work, Ensure simple/ adequate understanding and application of complex theories/technology

Build/Sustain a Confidential Relationship

Provide relevant/original product/Withstand errors and glitches, Stay Cool - Manage Conflict, Provide Updates when Available

Provide Ongoing, Relevant, and Usable Intelligence

Warning: Consultants, their product, process, methodology and networks increase the dimension of your intelligence risk:

- Establish a good fit

- Secure industry exclusivity where possible

Using the Innate Ability to Read Others

Extensive experience as a diplomat living and working in various parts of the world and many years of training and counseling diverse groups and individuals in the business world has made me impatient with the human tendency to *label* people. Very often such labels stick forever and assumed thoughts and behavior are assigned to people without any real analysis of circumstance. In the intelligence world, this practice can stop the effective gathering of clues, data, and information dead in its tracks.

For me, this problem is compounded by the enormous choice of *labeling tools* available. Computer-driven profiling is increasingly popular in the business world, made more so by promises of certainty with regard to employee productivity projections. He's a *Green*, she's *ENFJ*, they are *Left Brain*, he's a *Type A* are just some of the terms we hear. An extremely broad client base has necessitated interaction with individuals subscribing to greatly varying schools of thought and degrees of attachment to labeling tools of choice.

Making Conscious what is Innate

To meet clients and people in general on a common ground I have evolved a tool called SPICE™ that makes conscious the innate human ability to accurately read a person at a particular point in time. I believe this consciousness to be a prerequisite to whatever behavioral identification system is preferred. An awareness of SPICE should always be seen against the backdrop of the following considerations:

- People are in a constant state of complexity and change.

- Human behavior is dynamic and will respond proportionately to change.

- Emotional and social events will influence behaviour on a day to day basis.

- Identifying individual behavior at a certain point in time is fairer, more accurate and therefore preferable to permanently labeling/typecasting people.

- An insistence on certainty – doing and saying what is expected, safe or proven comes at a price. A common language of labels, brands, obligatory activities and image compliance stifles receptivity to external input, original thought and the evolution of innovative ideas.

- To err is human; mistakes in reading people can (and will) occur.

- Intelligence cannot be evaluated without evaluating its source.

The SPICE™ of Life

Be aware that people and their circumstances constantly change. People exist on Five levels:

1. Spiritual

2. Physical

3. Intellectual

4. Community

5. Emotional

It follows that people communicate and are communicated to on five levels. This innate human process is both conscious and sub-conscious.

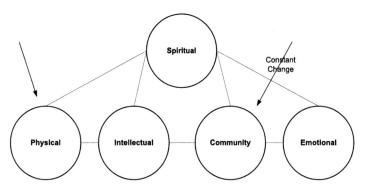

Figure 2.1: The five levels (SPICE) of human communication.

Few would argue that external input/stimulus on Physical and Community levels does not alter individual circumstance minute by minute, hour by hour and day by day. Logically, the interconnectivity between the five levels of being would enable us to safely say that all human beings are in a constant state of change. This fact necessitates a constant re-evaluation of people and situations, never assuming certainty or absolute predictability. It is very tempting at times to infer conclusions when we believe that we know someone or are familiar with certain situations and circumstances; to do so is to deny the existence of change, growth, or deterioration in others and ourselves.

This process does not have to be learned; it is innate and underway at all times. Making the process conscious allows for aware living as opposed to sterile existence. SPICE provides a simple window into individuals and groups, be they organizations, communities or countries.

> For every action there is an equal and opposite reaction.
>
> Sir Isaac Newton

Complete Spectrum Communication

The discussion of verbal and non-verbal ability in communication is important, as people are a source of intelligence/information. Reading people is crucial to intelligence and source evaluation. Carefully consider making the application of SPICE conscious in everyday conversation. Everyone consciously experiences unspoken communication at some point each day, especially with close friends and family. It is this innate process that continues without pause and without always penetrating consciousness, that must be explored, developed, made conscious and trusted.

In the intelligence arena, as we have seen, discovering and ultimately knowing a person is important in evaluating the intelligence they deliver. As time is not always an available commodity and because discretion is always a dictate of the intelligence operation, it is essential to read non-verbal language as efficiently and quickly as possible. Meeting a person is like being bombarded with dozens of clues. The ability to decipher them and piece together the puzzle as accurately as possible will make for excellent intelligence gathering and analysis.

It is vital that individuals and organizations know as much as possible about the people with whom they deal.

To make the process of outward and inward communicating conscious when interacting with people throughout the intelligence cycle, consider information/ data/intuition in the context of the person(s) who provide it at any given point in time. People and their circumstances change moment by moment, day by day, as does the context in which they communicate. Conversely, consciousness of the context in which we appear to others is equally important.

Remember: This process does not have to be learned, only made conscious.

Talk is only a pretext for other, subtler forms of communication. When the latter are inoperative, speech becomes dead. If two people are intent upon communicating with one another, it doesn't matter in the least how bewildering it becomes. People who insist on clarity and logic often fail in making themselves understood. They are always searching for a more perfect transmitter, deluded by the supposition that the mind is the only instrument for the exchange of thought. When one really begins to talk, one delivers himself. Words are thrown about recklessly, not counted like pennies. One doesn't care about grammatical or factual errors, contradictions, lies and so on. One talks. If you are talking to someone who knows how to listen, he understands perfectly, even though the words make no sense...

Henry Miller, *Sexus*.

Table 2.1: Examine People and Organizations on all Five Levels (SPICE)

Spiritual (Vision)

Management of uncertainty, risk taking, and flexibility

Ability to delegate, ask for help, tolerate, hope, dream, imagine, or choose unknown paths

Acceptance of failure, limitations, chance/luck, imperfection, and mishap

Physical (Endurance/Confidence)

Body language, gestures, appearance, race, gender, age health, hygiene, odor, eye contact, touch, voice, writing, documents.

Intellectual (Thinking)

Information processing, originality, creativity, performance management

Community (Values/Points of reference)

Education, career, marital status, family/friends, culture, interests, finances, religion/belief system

Emotional (Personality)

Character, confidence, history, baggage/scars

Behaviour: rational, active, passive, emotional

Attitude: caring, humorous, committed, confident, insecure, etc.

Caution:

- Be aware of the indicator(s)/yardstick(s) used to make any evaluation.

- Be aware of the differences that exist from society to society.

- Be aware of any recent changes in behavior? Factor in any known internal/external circumstances that might be at play.

- The greater the level of interaction, the greater the number of clues with which you will have to work. Keep your assessment dynamic and ongoing.

- Insecurity, low self esteem, organizational fatigue and employee burn out, not to speak of naïveté and inexperience, are just some of the factors that would hinder collection of valuable intelligence.

- Do not confuse potential with reality.

SPICE and Aware Communication

Vision, Endurance/Presentation, Ability/Competence, Values, and Passion are universally appreciated traits that reveal individuality consciously or subconsciously. An awareness of these traits enables conscious decoding of others/ourselves. Consider the subconscious process behind what we consciously refer to as *first impressions, love at first sight, great connections, like minds, good vibes, creepy, weird,* etc.

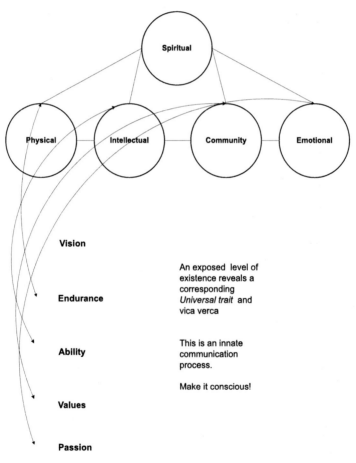

Figure 2.2: Vision, endurance, ability, values, and passion are traits that reveal individuality and can be used to decode others.

SPICE & the Professional Intelligence Profile

In addition to a talented fascination with clue spotting, making sense of random facts and the challenges of internal information delivery, the ideal intelligence professional requires a profile that includes:

- The capacity to juggle process **and** creativity – working accurately within set internal/external boundaries to discover undefined clues.

- A high degree of lateral and original thought – formulating relevant/logical theory.

- The capacity to keep focused on minutia while constantly aware of big-picture issues.

- Extensive industry-specific and general knowledge.

- An exceptional focus on set objectives and relationship building.

- A flexible, patient and tenacious approach to people and situations.

- Evolved research, analytical, and oral/written reporting expertise.

- The ability to interact on all levels of the corporate hierarchy.

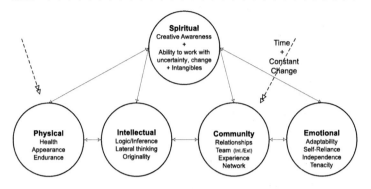

Figure 2.3: Consider SPICE to recognize the professional and personal attributes of the intelligence workers in terms of the desired profile.

The intelligence agent is someone who will be asked to transform this role into a permanent career choice. Cynically speaking, this person will be known as a corporate spy – a role that is not openly fashionable or even considered ethical. Like it or not, most business survival depends on the timely discovery of available intelligence; all global, national, industry and corporate details are relevant to the ongoing success of any organization. The competitive edge lies uniquely in the favorable balance of knowledge and preparedness to factor the same into workable strategies and plans at any point in time. It would be naïve in the extreme to ignore this fact.

The concerted efforts to achieve organizational/ business transparency and accountability at the present time will only serve to drive the professional intelligence agent and any related activity further underground.

Service Orientation

What would possess such a talented individual to apply a rare skill set for so little perceived reward?

The term *unsung hero* would best describe an accomplished intelligence agent. Tasks are carried out in a cloak of confidentiality: the task, the reason for the task, the steps followed to accomplish the tasks and even the benefit of successful task accomplishment remain the knowledge of a closed group of individuals. There is usually no public reward for success – certainly, no citation for meritorious service. More often than not the achievement remains unrecorded.

Should the intelligence agent step over the bounds of prevailing ethical, governance or best practices regulations, the "if you screw up, you're on your own" principle will have definite application. The message is clear: "We cannot and will not be implicated if you are exposed/caught!" Agents may be arrested in pursuance of illegal activity, only to find their Head Office denies all knowledge of their activity, just as surely, no physical trail will exist to prove otherwise. Available technology allows for an efficient across the board degree of external vigilance and forensic accuracy; coupled with the absence of a reliable safety net, this surely places an active agent at high risk.

It follows then, that the intelligence agent will almost constantly be traveling an uncertain path. Flexibility – the ability to improvise, alter plans and operate without instruction – the capacity to trust and be trusted, an acceptance of limitations, a reliance on intuition, and the ability to not lose sight of a specific mandate are qualities that are essential to survival in the field.

It is obvious that implicit faith in the task giver's instructions and unquestioning obedience are the order of the day.

Bridging Barriers

The global interconnectivity of culture, background, ability, technology and business greatly adds to the task of the intelligence agent. No two people think alike, meaning that interpretation, value/belief systems and agendas will change form person to person and place to place. The task of the intelligence agent is to play different games with different rules to accurately determine what is meant by whom at any specific point in time.

The ability to subjectively assess available information, data, and people while simultaneously using objective analytical expertise to connect random clues with intelligence objectives that are relevant to the given mandate will ultimately define the established intelligence expertise.

Discovery vs. Spying

It must be stressed that illegal/unethical corporate spying is not advocated. There is sufficient available information for discovery in the public domain that will indicate *interesting* developments in the intelligence target arena.

Understanding Behavior - Personality Types Made Simple

The behavior of individuals, groups, or nations will always have distinct consequences. A consideration of SPICE illustrates that people and situations change continually, change bringing with it inevitable cause and effect. This being true, an open mind when evaluating intelligence and formulating a response to people and situations, will allow for a clearer reflection, understanding and use of available intelligence.

Identifying and responding to *specific behavior* is less complicated and more useful than permanently labeling the people involved in its procurement. While people do have definite character traits, it is a dangerous practice to assume or infer that they will *always* behave in a certain way just because they did so in the past.

Rather than selecting one of the many excellent behavioral type models, I have outlined the four underlying character states that I believe underpin all human behavior in infinitely variable combinations.

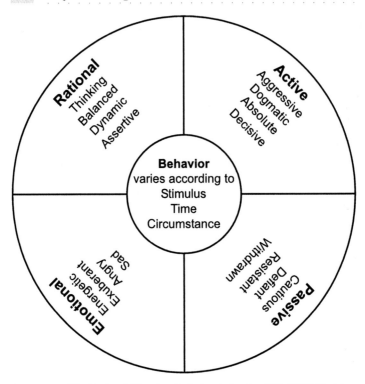

Figure 2.4: The Rational, Emotional, Active & Passive (REAP™) Model

The Rational State

The **Rational State** is evidence of the balanced evolution of the human condition at any given time. It reflects logical processing of emotion, past conditioning, learning, needs and desires in the light of external stimuli and circumstances. Given that people display all these traits (REAP) to varying degrees all of the time, if a person is in a rational state he or she can be said to be *thinking* at that particular moment. It is then hard not to accept that being *mostly rational* would be preferable to being *mostly active*, *mostly emotional* or *mostly passive*.

Rationality ideally manages innate and learned ability to best advantage. In the rational state, one may choose to enter active, emotional or passive states for strategic purposes. This would intrinsically illustrate the difference between responding and reacting to people and situations:

- **Rationally Active -** Deciding for a specific reason (time, budget constraints, etc.) that a temporarily aggressive or dominant approach will be followed. In business, top-down decisions, cutbacks, and other imposed circumstances would be examples of active behaviour. In the business and intelligence worlds, it may at times be necessary to decide unilaterally when faced with pressure, diverse points of view and indecisive players.

- **Rationally Emotional -** Caring (nurturing, concerned, protective when necessary), Exuberant (enthusiastic, fun-loving, witty but not irresponsible joker-type behaviour), and Angry (release of tension/expression of displeasure in a well-directed and appropriate manner, not uncontrolled temper, rage, or violence).

- **Rationally Passive -** Time-out, a well earned rest (not procrastination or refusal to take responsibility for one's own well-being or that of others); Conscious decision not to get involved in a specific situation after weighing the pros and cons.

Table 2.2: Rationally versus Emotionally-Secured Intelligence

Rationally-Secured Intelligence	*Emotionally/Actively/ Passively-Secured Intelligence*
- Balanced - Verified - Dynamic/objective - Relevant - Goal oriented - Big Picture - Thought provoking /interesting - Action oriented (consequential)	- Competitive/potentially inaccurate - Ambiguous - Rigid/subjective - Isolated - Random - One dimensional - Off-putting/offensive - Stagnant/boring

The Active State

Most people have an aspect of conditioning and experience that supports their credos, dogmas and beliefs. In its raw state this trait is unequivocal in its expression and leaves no room for any other point of view – it criticizes, imposes upon, offends and judges others. On a positive note, the active state evidences the drive and focus that achievers need to ensure task completion.

Intelligence secured from Active State (Predominant) - Caution!

Potentially:

- Competitively inspired

- Unquestioning/2nd hand opinions

- High degree of inference - Relying on past experience rather than the interpretation of current facts

- Unequivocal statements/smugness/self righteousness/complacent

- Hasty decisions without weighing the options

- Impatience; with poor listening skills

- Controlling and overbearing manner in team scenarios, shutting out potentially useful input

- Provokes active, emotional or passive behaviour

The Emotional State

Emotion is a crucial part of our personality that is always present. It should not be the overriding factor in our thinking, decision making or interaction with others. Intelligence secured on an emotional (unthinking) basis may limit the value or damage the effectiveness of an overall contribution.

- *Exuberance* is the creative and unfettered side of the human personality that reflects happiness, fun, charm and light-heartedness. When overly used by an individual he or she could be considered irresponsible or flippant.

- *Service Orientation/Caring* is that aspect of our personality that expresses our concern for others. Taken to the extreme, it may evidence a paternalistic/controlling attitude that in the intelligence/business world will stifle healthy input and innovative thought in those exposed to this behaviour for prolonged periods of time.

- *Anger* is the built-in human *safety valve*. A degree of *venting* or *letting off steam* is desirable. Angry energy accumulated, when properly channelled, is visible through successful sporting and artistic achievement, for example. When anger is allowed to run unchecked it will provoke either like behaviour (Emotional), decisive confrontation (Active), withdrawal (Passive) or hopefully reason (Rational).

Intelligence secured from Emotional State (Predominant) - Caution!

Potentially:

- Biased

- Reactive/illogical/crisis driven

- Coloured by non related events/baggage/ history

- Unfocused/clouded

- Undue weight attached to minor side issues

- Unverified

- Overly insistent

- Provokes emotional, active or passive behaviour

The Passive State

Passivity is indicative of the armour we have to protect ourselves from harm/hurt. It allows for privacy and the recharging of batteries. If overly used, it can become a crutch that manifests itself in excessive shyness, whining, refusal to accept responsibility, procrastination or daydreaming.

A withdrawn or self conscious person is patently passive while other variations are harder to spot and their behaviour is often mistaken for rational, active or emotional. These individuals are the biggest threat to the intelligence process; they usually deflect attention from themselves by identifying the faults of others or the process and often are evidence of an extremely active and rational delivery style. The easiest way to unmask this behaviour is to ask how often action or results came about as result of the person's actions.

Intelligence secured from Passive State (Predominant) - Caution!

Potentially:

- Non existent

- Inaccurate

- Misleading

- Disguised/misstated

- Underplayed/mediocre

- Compliant (the *"yes man"* syndrome, feeding expectations)

- Too little too late

- Provokes passive, active or emotional behaviour

The Individual in the Intelligence Process

There are three distinct roles in the intelligence process:

1. **The Collector** - Gathers all specific information wherever it may be found.

2. **The Processor** - Analyzes and evaluates the information on its own merits.

3. **The Decision/Policy Maker** - Uses the processed information to formulate policy and to determine possible action.

As we have seen, the intelligence process requires walking an unknown path; the intelligence team member must be flexible and willing to proceed with discretion on a situation-by-situation or person-by-person basis. The capacity of the individual to work with uncertainty relates directly to how effective he or she will be as an intelligence worker.

Although obtaining and evaluating information is difficult, most employees, to varying degrees, should meet the requirements for collecting and analyzing intelligence:

- Analytical/flexible thinking with research and communication ability

- A strong interest in an industry or a company's products and activity

- A proven fit on a social and personal level with the company

- A willingness to grow with or invest in the company

- A clear service orientation

Human impressions, experiences and individual events influence the collection of information and the process of analysis. A sense of vision and reliance on intuition is necessary to interpret or forecast events. Known statistics are generally insufficient for policy creation; constant renewal and verification is necessary to obtain an accurate picture of their development in the context of politics, economics, cultural matters and attitudes, etc.

An organization that places employees in the best possible position to consider options, exercise choice and understand what it is to be part of the collective corporate responsibility will, of necessity, access the best intelligence.

While not part of a formal job description, collecting and processing information is a potential role for most company members.

The servant must think earnestly of the business of his employer... when thinking arises above concern for your own welfare, wisdom, which is independent of thought appears.

Miyamoto Musashi

The Collector - An Intelligence Gatherer

In addition to job specific duties, Sales, Marketing, Field Service, Customer Service, Account Management, Technical Service and IT people are well placed to provide information and advice to policy makers. Their input is crucial when goals and action plans are considered and decided.

Individual skill in interpreting and contextualizing the information/data/statistics provided will assist in determining residual value. This ability is in direct relation to the external knowledge the employee has acquired regarding the industry, product, client or country in question.

Information + Context + Interpretation/Prediction = Intelligence

There are inherent dangers in the process of accessing this intelligence:

- Perceived reluctance of Head Office/Top Management to act on the information provided may result in resentment in the collector.

- There is a reluctance of the collector to *let go* once the information has been provided.

- There may be conflicting opinions/interference from other (especially senior) organizational members.

- Bureaucracy and a poor/slow communication procedure may lead to outdated information.

The importance attached to the collector's input is dependent on any number of factors:

- Reputation in decision-making circles

- Reputation for reliability/initiative

- Service orientation

- Ability to accept the bigger picture

- Collaborative relationship building with relevant organization players in the operational area

- Integrity/Self Esteem/Courage

- Efficient communication competencies - written/oral

Information + Context + Interpretation/Prediction + Perceived Relevance = Useful Intelligence

Accurate and relevant information must be provided to minimize the discrepancy between actual conditions in a given environment and that held by policy makers. Knowledge of trends, attitudes and intentions on a social, political, economic, military and corporate level is critical if the right decisions are to be made. The enormity of individual responsibility in this regard is evident.

The collector/information provider will more often than not be required to sell the intelligence upward – Analysts, planners and top management need to know why they should act on the material provided. If this task is accepted as an integral part of the process, individual motivation to continue inputting intelligence will not be put at risk. (See Chapter 7 for more details.)

The Intelligence Analyst/Processor

The analyst has the task of making sense of the intelligence provided by the collector. There are three vital parts to this process.

Acknowledgement of the collector

In any workplace relationship, recognition of work done remains the single most important motivating factor. This is important, as the collection process requires initiative and the definite choice of an individual to act in the best interest of the organization - especially true when this role is not part of the individual's written job description. Feedback should be provided wherever possible. If for big picture reasons feedback is not possible, this should be clearly explained to the collector either on each specific occasion of as part of a general management policy.

Validation is necessary for securing individual contribution.

Evaluation and analysis of the intelligence received

Placing the intelligence in the context of the gatherer (SPICE) and integrating it with known facts and existing information is the next step. The exercise, if performed thoroughly, is a valuable check on the tendency or temptation to react rather than respond to input received. Care must be taken to work quickly, minimizing the delay between reception and recommendation. Stale intelligence is worse than no intelligence as expiration of relevance will waste the cost of the process to date, lose the advantage of foreknowledge and potentially demotivate the gatherer.

Analysis focused on ascertaining the impact and use of the material must be conducted with every human and technical resource available. Clear trends, theories, etc. need to be evolved from the intelligence provided. Should the gatherer have already completed this process, it is suggested that a recheck in relation to larger organizational circumstances be undertaken. All theories must reflect a conscious interpretation of the value, cultural and socio-economic context in which they were discovered as well as the corresponding context in which they will have an expected impact.

Useful Intelligence + Organizational Context + Benefit/Consequence = Relevant Intelligence Recommendation

Recommendations to the policy maker

At this point an intelligence *product* is delivered to the decision makers. The assumption would be that organizational interest would be best served by the analyst's recommendation that would not have been made unless all checks and balances have been carried out.

The report should clearly state the degree to which it has been checked and is complete, the level of unverified content, as well as the circumstances surrounding collection, time constraints and the like.

The Decision/Policy Maker - The End User

The policy or decision maker is the first *end-user* or eventual client in the intelligence cycle. This individual must assess the analyst's recommendations and measure the value of the intelligence together with the potential impact of use or non-use in the context the global organizational priorities. The underlying complexity of the tasks facing the various players involved in the intelligence cycle makes this a world of uncertainty and risk that is daunting to many. Those who make decisions based on intelligence collected and analyzed usually bear responsibility for the entire process.

Surrendering to the bigger picture!

While all organizational intelligence players ideally need to be kept in the informational loop, complex corporate, industrial, national and intergovernmental factors might be classified and for security or strategic reasons may be unavailable for general consumption.

For these and other reasons, however strange it may seem, the valuable intelligence collected may not be used. The policy maker bears the ultimate responsibility and has the final say in this regard. Both the collector and processor need to accept this as a cardinal rule in the intelligence world.

Ensuring mutual big picture understanding between all the players is critical if intelligence relevance is to be established on a continuous basis.

**Relevant Intelligence Recommendation +
Organizational Impact + Industry Context =
Effective Policy Adjustment**

The responsibility of making decisions that have long and potentially costly effects (as well as accountability to a higher authority) should not be ignored as a sensitive factor in the intelligence process. Given that most people err on the side of caution, intelligence will traditionally be a hard sell if the decision maker perceives the new intelligence as:

- Controversial or a departure from current objectives

- In conflict with a preferred approach

- Fuelling internal dissent

- Premature – Pending legislation and or bigger picture decisions

- Having no precedent

- Calling for action beyond the scope of budgetary constraints

- Discordant with Board/Group/Hierarchical priorities

- Leading the organization to involvement in potentially illegal/unethical activities

Further factors for consideration would be centered on the personal attributes of the decision maker that might negatively affect the reception of new intelligence:

- Preference for alternative choice/solution/ scenario

- Subjective circumstance/mind set/value system at any point in time

- Level of competence/interest/initiative

- Personal career path/risk/power hoarding

- Corporate resentment/baggage

Corporate Group Decision-Making

The global economy is characterized by multi-national conglomerates managing widespread operations that cross political, social and cultural boundaries. This fact, coupled with the prevalent merger/buyout scenarios that occur on a daily basis, leads to many corporate cultures that are dictated by a Head Office far removed from a specific product or service context. Many top management figures are obliged to make decisions that take group or holding company process, politics/alliances, and instruction into account.

It is suggested that this state of affairs should not change the basic approach to good intelligence. True leaders with a strong service orientation will not be daunted by the challenge of selling vital intelligence upward.

An awareness of the dangers of remote/isolated decisions, the risk of message distortion and bottlenecks in the communication process, and excessive time elapse should be ever present.

The decision maker, as the first end user, is an integral part of the intelligence process and as such should not require false promises of certainty and fudged realities. The tendency to feed decision makers, in their capacity as the internal client, what they want to hear, as opposed to what they need to hear, should be avoided. In the same spirit, there should be no harm in being wrong. A dynamic, decentralized decision-making process will allow for ongoing corroboration, correction and flexibility.

Effective Policy Adjustment + Uncertainty Demystified + Conscious Thinking + Leadership + Ripple Effect = Intelligence Awareness

Figure 3.1: The inclusive approach to decision making.

Leadership - The Decision to Serve!

Leadership in the Intelligence world involves the individual ability to:

Perceive an Opportunity

Be Aware
An opportunity is presented or discovered.

Make a Choice
(A Critical Step)

Be Decisive
The opportunity is assessed, and the decision is made to accept the challenge with all attendant risks.

Apply Knowledge/Ability/Original thought/Creativity

Be Competent
The full application of ability and resources is brought to bear to achieve a set objective(s). Stimulation is brought on by the desire to serve/the challenge presented.

Achieve Buy-In

Collaborate

The extent of leadership responsibility becomes apparent: the importance of relationships, the need to communicate with integrity and the conscious decision to remain at once both subjective and objective to better sell benefits and consequences individually and collectively.

Manage Uncertainty

Be Dynamic/Flexible

Ensuring team-performance rather than the imposition of will is preferable . Commitment is critical to ensuring a workable and relevant solution. Guidance, mentoring and effective channels of communication ensure overall team/client contribution, efficiency and contentment.

Delegation/acceptance of limitation/imperfection where necessary, trusting, asking for help, acknowledging others, taking risks, re-evaluating/defining objectives will lead to:

Ongoing Intelligence Accuracy and Relevance

The Intelligence Environment & Individual/ Team Motivation

Reward & Acknowledgement

As we have seen, business intelligence is measured on the ability to provide new and unknown knowledge, ideas, concepts and information or data that will advance the organization on any level of its operation.

Motivation in the form of reward and acknowledgement usually ensures that individuals and teams embrace the intelligence role. This factor often creates complicated scenarios that must be consciously addressed to ensure ongoing intelligence gathering, analysis, decision making and the consequent free organizational knowledge flow.

Inherent in the human condition is the desire to please – to provide what the internal or external client wants, not what he or she needs. There is also a very real danger that the higher the reward or acknowledgement, the greater the risk that the intelligence process will become transactional (set rewards for set intelligence task achievements). This trend would present a very real danger in the form of the natural human impulse to secure rewards or management/executive approval rather than deliver what might be perceived as unwelcome intelligence, resulting in systemic failure of the entire foundation of the process. Contrived intelligence will

- Become limited in scope, rejecting the random/ unproven

- Avoid striking a discordant/contrary note with existing policy

- Confirm anticipated results

- Strive for certainty and adhere to traditional (what works) patterns

- Consciously/sub-consciously feed hierarchical egos

- Manipulate desired outcomes

It is recommended that motivation in the form of reward or acknowledgement be kept fluid (defined person by person, situation by situation) dependent on

- Management awareness that intuition, randomness and uncertainty define good intelligence

- Clear, yet flexible identification of priority areas for collection, as well as critical performance indicators

- Loose linkage of collection capacity (as opposed to collection priorities) to the business plan

- Acceptance that occasional inaccuracy and lack of relevance are part of the game and should not be obstacles to future exploration

- Subjective decisions set against objective organizational context/dynamics to strategically apportion tangible or intangible rewards

- Appreciation and understanding that a fluid organizational intelligence or knowledge culture directly impacts on the intelligence individual/ team satisfaction, performance and sense of belonging and loyalty

The ideal organizational reward continuum will (wherever possible) reflect

- Management awareness of intelligence input, origins and significance

- A realistic business plan with key performance area guidelines and critical performance indicators agreed to by relevant teams and individuals

- Actual accommodation or use of intelligence provided

- Appropriate feedback in relation to agreed individual and team performance indicators

- Adequate tangible and intangible rewards and acknowledgement

- Appropriate and strategic recognition of the final intelligence product in real organizational terms

- Encouragement of further input

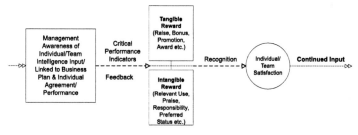

Figure 3.2: The Organizational Intelligence Reward Continuum

Tangible Reward

Individual organizational process and best practices as well as strategic circumstance will determine what level of tangible reward is appropriate for excellence in the intelligence process. Typically, financial recompense is always welcome but does not always factor in the emotional and community aspects of individual and team make-up. It cannot be denied, however, that a raise, bonus or promotion as recompense for a job well done will always be a factor in measuring personal satisfaction.

Caveat:

- This type of reward creates a precedent and raises levels of expectation

- Overt financial reward publicly alerts an onlooker to the value of the intelligence provided at any point in time – Not always the best strategic move!

- A potential sense of competition between team members may supplant intelligence or knowledge objectives in individual prioritization

Intangible Reward

If it is accepted that a successful career is the full and enjoyable use of innate and learned abilities in a dynamic environment, then perhaps the best forms of intangible reward would be those that accommodate these elements, fostering a meaningful sense of contribution and belonging or loyalty. Possible intangible rewards will include

Primary:

- Relevant use of the intelligence product

- Feedback as to absorption of the intelligence where appropriate/circumspect

- Increased intelligence responsibility

- Specialized mandate

- Specific praise - Recognition of individual or team competencies involved in gathering, analyzing and processing the intelligence

Secondary:

- Active support and engagement of management in the intelligence process

- Adequate framework – Resources, budget, people, current IT process/tools, etc. to ensure quality deliverables

- Ongoing process review and fine-tuning

- Relevant guidance or training

- Circumspect best practice and efficiency measurement guidelines

- Sustained organizational awareness

Feedback

Constructive feedback is an easy and cost-effective motivational tool. Rather than leaving an individual team to find their own way, ongoing availability of a guide, mentor or sounding board goes a long way to rewarding or acknowledging good work.

In the intelligence/knowledge arena the following areas of assistance should be considered:

- Measured success of deliverables

- Briefing as to current and projected requirements

- Guidelines for enhanced gathering, analysis practicalities, focus, techniques, new methodology, etc.

- Discussion of the pros and cons of risk and realistic/unrealistic expectations

- Personal interaction, communication and reporting skill enhancement – New ideas, innovation, etc. that represent a departure from traditional or actual trends need to be sold internally

- The value of balancing process and creativity – Exploring unknown territory within the capacity of the organization to absorb new thinking

- The relevant and essential use of new information processing technology

The *Managing* Manager

The underlying attitude of the manager toward the employee is pivotal in creating a ripple effect of intelligence awareness in any organization.

To ensure that full employee intelligence potential is accessed, every manager should demonstrate ability to

- Understand individual roles in the specific workplace

- Accept the importance of the intelligence awareness profile

- Hire the right people for the right positions

- Act as a mentoring supervisor

- Access the full participation of the employee in terms of team and corporate objectives

- Manage the input, co-ordination and distribution of intelligence gathered

In this way, the manager enables the organization to build on its investment and create suitable conditions for meeting corporate objectives. I believe this traditional role has been eroded over the past fifteen years or so. The newly-appointed manager today finds the title brings three times the workload, and responsibility for any number of performance reviews. The latter, more often than not, end up vague, politically correct documents that leave employees feeling unrecognized and frustrated. Remote management, coupled with transient employees and the climate of endless buyouts, mergers, downsizing, terminations and *lettings go*, results in a dispirited work force suffering from what is loosely defined as *Organizational Fatigue*.

The manager should see the employee as an investment!

If an employee leaves, for whatever reason, or does not produce more than his or her annual salary plus the approximately 33.3% additional benefit/training/cost layout, the employer has effectively made a bad investment and the company has lost money. The loss of corporate knowledge and risk of an intelligence leak is self-evident.

FACTOID: When senior executives were asked which skills were the more difficult to attract and retain, 50% said people with technical skills, and 36% said people who were flexible and adaptable.

While 68% felt that it is important to develop existing employees, most felt that retaining those people was a major challenge. **When employees do leave, 69% move to competitors in the same business.**

Source: Accenture

Using the Intelligence Profile in the Hiring Process

Most companies have a specific hiring/recruiting policy and procedure. The following guidelines are intended to enhance/underscore the awareness of those involved as to the importance of the new hire as a corporate intelligence resource.

Exploring Intelligence Awareness Potential - Begin at the Beginning

A *thinking hiring policy* will allow the recruitment of *thinking people.*

Awareness at recruitment level as to the common employee **role** of asset protector, information gatherer, and processor in as many positions as possible, would strengthen the fabric of any organization. Assess ability to:

- **Perceive the intelligence environment.** Check attitude and experience regarding information gathering and asset protection?

- **Identify/allocate/assume individual intelligence responsibility.** What is the intelligence potential and experience of the individual?

- **Take appropriate action.** What approach would be followed in an intelligence scenario?

- **Reach a satisfactory conclusion.** What level of detail would be brought to an intelligence task?

About 28 per cent of the 250,000 employee background checks that InfoMart conducts every month yield discrepancies or problems, and more than 10 per cent uncover criminal histories. For foreign-born workers, however, hits are rarer: about 6 per cent. Those workers are also more likely to have lied about their education and employment histories than have covered up a criminal past.

Blair Cohen, Info mart, Atlanta.
Source: *Globe & Mail,* 5 November 2001

Additional tips:

- If using an outside consultant, be clear as to the intelligence profile requirements of the prospective hire. Ongoing briefing/input/ feedback would be useful if the right people are to be secured for the right positions.

- Use in-house intelligence awareness tools as far as possible to facilitate background, security and reference checks. These are fallible components of the hiring process - There are no guarantees that a background check has been exhaustive.

- A system inclusive of local and international background checking procedures should be evolved for every organization. Profile trends, employee history/behavior and an ex-employee's intended or present place of employment, etc. should ideally be the type of information that is recorded, analyzed and updated on a regular basis.

- Remember that background checks reflect recorded information data only. Do not abandon rational/emotional input (SPICE).

Evaluating Organizations

Evaluating organizations, corporations and what they represent in the business world depends on understanding the people who work for the organization, individually and collectively. Employee contentment or discontent impacts on the collective corporate wellbeing in many ways, not least being the image of the organization that is projected externally. Close examination of outward corporate representation will reveal what is going on internally. Routine scrutiny (using SPICE) of any organization is especially relevant in the light of a volatile global economy and socio-political developments with consequent downsizing, mergers, restructuring, etc.

Using SPICE to Recognize Corporate Malaise

People's behavior will always provide clues as to the health of a company. Failure to ascertain internally or externally whether problematic behavior is personal or organizational in nature may result in costly business transactions, financial loss and disastrous associations. An ongoing awareness of changing scenarios and their consequent impact is essential in maintaining the competitive edge.

Organizational Fatigue and *Burnout* are imprecise concepts that are perhaps the most direct indicators that something serious is amiss within a company. They commonly describe an individual or group *mechanism* that comes into play when perceptions of threat, fear, or loss become prevalent in the business world. Fatigue levels relate directly to performance and vulnerability of individuals and groups within the company.

Internal Examination:

An organizational diagnostic to assess:

- Company or departmental information-gathering efficiency

- Company or departmental vulnerability to external information gathering

- Organizational *depth* - the employee sense of loyalty and belonging

External Examination:

- Assessing the depth of potential and existing client relationships

- Assessing competitor efficiency

- Assessing the viability of partnerships and associations

- Assessing supplier efficiency and loyalty

- Evaluating and confirming information or data received

Characteristics of a Healthy Organization – Potential Clues

- A high degree of client satisfaction

- Consistent profit or dividend

- New product development

- Sound product or service reputation

- Solid and ethical business practice

- An energized and enthusiastic atmosphere

- Positive and productive employees

- Low rate of attrition - productive and loyal personnel remain with the company

- Enthusiasm in the face of misfortune

- Pro-active and innovative managerial behavior

- Open and direct communication on all levels

- Relevant diversification and technological updates

- Ongoing employee development

Symptoms of an Unhealthy Company - Potential Clues

(Early Stages)

- General anxiety and low morale

- Resistance and inertia with regard to new initiatives

- Lack of prioritization with regard to work load

- Decreased productivity and inferior work

- Procrastination

- Lack of punctuality

- Increased demand for leave

- Complaints or defeatism; creating a negative vision

- Lack of self motivation; the inability to work alone

- Increased irritability and sensitivity; the *"poor me"* (or victim) syndrome

(Advanced stages)

- Irrational fear; revolt; aggression

- Increased absenteeism or loss of work days

- Obvious signs of alcohol and substance abuse

- Increased illness among employees

- Increased medical compensation claims

- Increased conflict

- Avoidance of decision making and initiative

- *Quit and Stay* syndrome

- Resignation (Attrition), especially among the most valued employees

- Client dissatisfaction

- Noticeable decrease in productivity (allow for cause and effect time elapse)

- Loss of profit

Table 4.1: The *Individual* and the Unhealthy Organization	
Temporary Symptoms	
Physical	**Psychological**
- Tension headaches - Bowel disorders - Weight fluctuation - Sleep irregularities - Eating irregularities - Sexual dysfunction - Skin problems - Muscular aches	- Frustration - Irritability - Anxiety - Depression - Mood swings - Withdrawn/passive behavior - Interpersonal problems - Substance abuse
Long-Term Symptoms	
Physical	**Psychological**

- Nervous body language
- Hair loss
- Heart disease
- Strokes
- Ulcers
- Immune system deficiency
	- Acute depression
	- Violent behavior
	- Chronic substance abuse
	- Suicidal tendencies
	- Carelessness resulting in
	  accidents
	- Psychological disorders/
	  neurosis

Table 4.2: The *Team* and the Unhealthy Organization	
General Symptoms	
Physical	**Psychological**
- Decrease in contact between members - Lack of group cohesion - Discord and conflict - Complaints from members - Disloyalty - Lack of new initiative - Aggressive resistance to management - Increased failure to meet objectives - Missed deadlines	- Attitude problems - Group neurosis - Anger - Passivity - Us versus Them syndrome - Paranoia - Insecurity - Inability to focus on tasks - General group dysfunction

The Diagnostic

A careful consideration of symptoms and causes similar to those in the sample survey, taking time to explore each step, should uncover useful information or data about any organization that will enable efficient decision making.

An investigative checklist will evaluate appropriate areas of the company and individual as well as alerting the intelligence gatherer to various areas that might warrant investigation. This exercise will be particularly useful in directing management to areas of potential interest that may have been overlooked in previous strategic analysis.

Once again, the dangers of locking into a fixed template-type analysis should be avoided.

Stay Alert for Potential Intelligence

Information with regard to a specific company:

- Management

- Employee wellness issues

- Clients

- Products

- Finances and statistics

- Future

How the information or data impacts on the collecting individual or company

- Potential advantage: competitive, instructional, or warning

- Industry alert

- Source of new recruits

- New clients

- Regional economic or socio-political impact

Caution

- Before concluding that what may be isolated or temporary incidents of employee dissatisfaction are symptoms of burn out or organizational fatigue, check for indicators of positive and healthy employee commitment.

- It is important to bring as many possible scenarios into play before making a final assessment of what it is that actually constitutes the intelligence gathered. Remember that intelligence is a collection of clues pointing toward a possible future event or evolution of circumstance.

Organizational Fatigue: Sample Check list/Survey

In addition to a careful consideration of **SPICE**, pay specific attention to the following pointers to the health of an organization or individual at any point in time:

Personal Interaction/Experience:

* Do you perceive there to be conflict in the organization?

* Have others made mention of conflict or lack of harmony in the organization?

* Do members of the organization complain externally or behave in a disloyal fashion?

* Have they regularly made negative comments regarding their superiors?

* Do junior members behave differently or hypocritically in the presence of their superiors?

* In meetings do you detect individual or team apathy, or a failure to take initiative?

* Have you noticed an *Us* vs *Them* scenario (divisions)?

* Are there performance issues: delivery dates, high quality service, etc.?

* In your opinion, are the attributes or skills of individuals and teams fully accessed to meet the achievement goals?

Check the Physical Working Conditions/ Environment:

- Lack of security on social, economic and political levels

- Pressure brought about by technological developments; lack of privacy

- Less than ideal working conditions; for example, sterility, noise/air/electronic pollution, insufficient natural light, inadequate equipment, etc.

Organizational Issues:

- Perceived lack of opportunity for career advancement

- Random planning and management

- Dissatisfaction with organizational relationships

- Dissatisfaction or difficulty with allocated tasks

- Unclear job description, or onerous workload

- Discomfort with structure, procedure, objectives and management style

- Inadequate channels of communication

Possible Change-Related Factors:

- Innovation and rapid growth

- Redundancy of product; client loss; downsizing; survivor syndrome leading to mistrust or cynicism

- Uncertainty as to personal or group role

- Isolation or loss of unique identity in the company hierarchy

- Uncertainty as to performance ability

- Short-staffing leading to added workload

- A lack of communication as to the reasons for change initiatives

- A perception that coercion and bullying tactics are being used

Corporate Wellness Program for Organizational and Environmental Change

- There is recognition and identification of problem areas

- Policy and procedure are openly communicated to employees, ensuring company cohesiveness

- There are ongoing team-building, diversity, change, growth and stress management enhancement programs

- There are enabling tools provided for realistic individual or team self-assessments leading to the positive giving and receiving of feedback

- Care is taken to provide a healthy, comfortable and safe working environment

- Clear and adequate avenues for career advancement are set in place

- Career development programs have been implemented

- Relevant training programs have been evolved in collaboration with employees

- Collaboration with employees becomes part of the company culture

- There are clearly defined job descriptions and workloads

- Flexibility and adaptability are *sold* to employees as vehicles for accessing a competitive advantage

The Cost of Organizational Fatigue

- Conscious information or data leakage

- Damage to the company reputation

- Unconscious sabotage - a *don't care* attitude

- Company vulnerability to espionage

- Loss of man hours

- Non involvement in initiatives

- Deadwood employees

- Loss of qualified employees

- Wasted investment in employees

- De-motivation of other employees

- *Quit & Stay* Mentality

- Negligence, damage, betrayal

- Increased absenteeism

- Lack of employee development

- Medical compensation claims

Individuals may respond actively, passively or emotionally to organizational fatigue. The repression of inner feelings of stress, resentment and anger over an extended period of time may result in violent confrontation, resignation or nervous collapse. From the outset, a ripple effect will be at work that will eventually create a toxic operational environment.

Intelligence & Thinking Relationships

A healthy and relevant relationship will withstand many ups and downs. We are talking about *Loyalty!* If loyalty is present in a business relationship, individuals will comfortably discuss most industry, product developments, and any perceived threats or unusual behavior that might be relevant to industry or organizational well being.

In any relationship, simple acknowledgement of individuality ensures that all parties are recognized and appreciated for who they are. People are happiest when they are using *all* innate and learned ability. It is logical that a business relationship will benefit if each party to the relationship is

- Aware of his or her own reason for being in the relationship.

- Aware of his or her ability and its continued relevance to the relationship.

- Aware that all relationships require nurturing.

- Aware of bottom-line business objectives.

- Recognized for individual contribution.

In all business relationships, make a conscious effort to

- Show genuine interest.

- Promote dialogue that provides clarity.

- Ask questions to secure more detail (who/time/place/circumstance).

- Give feedback wherever discretion allows. This is often the best way of expressing appreciation.

- Express thanks.

A constant and loyal relationship is a valuable corporate commodity. Ensure all intelligence gathered is entered into the information system!

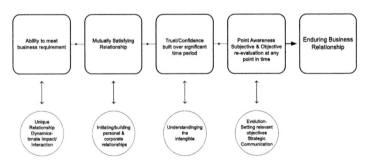

Figure 5.1: The Relationship Dynamics Theory

The Intelligence Network & Relationship Management

Relationship building is the conscious process of managing individual impact on human interaction. Relationships are a given in life, albeit in an often passive or unconscious mode. Managing this impact positively will bring us to a more effective level of interaction in business and a higher rate of focused or random intelligence goal achievement.

Developing a personal attitude of success is vital to effective business relationships. A constant and positive projection of yourself, your ability and the service you provide will inspire a client/company/source to appreciate your ability, personality and values and allow trust to become a natural part of the equation. If it is not pleasant or advantageous to be in your company, there will be little reason to have a relationship.

A healthy relationship that allows the effective exchange of information will be evidenced by four simple factors:

Mutual Liking
Mutual Respect
Mutual Awareness of Professional Expertise

+

Easy Access

- *Making contact with informed sources* is what directly concerns you. In the competitive business world, experience has shown that healthy personal relationships impact positively on personal and corporate objectives. Well-disposed colleagues, employers, clients and even friends will be inclined to build a relationship of confidence and trust and will refer to your expertise and knowledge when necessary. Conversely, this will open the door to a two-way exchange of information. The more frequently this exchange takes place, the less likely you will be considered to have an agenda; this is important as ulterior motives are readily transparent. Good relationships are not built in a day and can only be measured in terms of personal effort.

- Relationships are a permanent factor in the pursuit of accurate and relevant intelligence. It is not at any point suggested that a mercenary or transactional approach to relationship building or that insincere social posturing should take place. If interested in a certain field, involvement in related areas is natural. Take advantage of what there is to be learned from those around you.

**Relationships + Openness + Awareness =
Preparedness for Intelligence Gathering**

Above all, avoid being transactional in your approach to business relationships!

Initiating an Effective Intelligence Relationship

Establish liking and respect

Conversation is important to relationship building. In business, small talk provides a window to your personality and greatly assists in establishing compatibility. (SPICE)

- Chance meetings and remarks present opportunities. Be ready to discuss interests, preferences and express opinions, etc. to provoke a meaningful interaction that might result in fortuitous information.

- Asking and answering relevant questions will make for easy conversation. Responses to questions or opinions provide vital clues and insight to establishing/maintaining a fit/qualifying a potential source.

- Showing an interest in others is the most effective form of individual acknowledgement. Providing positive feedback reinforces trust.

- Be collaborative rather than dismissive when presented with half-developed theories and disjointed information.

- Freely offer opinions and business solutions if the occasion arises.

- Avoid insincere and flippant conversation; be your natural self! At large gatherings, be mindful that you are not overheard repeating the same *schtik* over and over again!

- Be cautious in relating anecdotes and stories that would cast doubt on your ethics or morals.

- Always carry your business card with you and exchange cards whenever possible. Of all the personal marketing tools, this item is the least likely to hit the trashcan. Your card should be up to date and specify the exact service you provide.

- Where appropriate, ask for something: an appointment, more information, a referral, an appropriate time to call again, etc.

- A positive attitude is contagious - people readily perceive the success you enjoy and your enthusiasm for your career and will be pleased to talk to you.

Source Identification and Subsequent Interaction

- Define a specific objective: what or who is the desired goal?

- Decide on your message: what distinguishes you from the next person? Prepare and be comfortable with a message that will clearly, correctly and concisely describe you, your industry position and how you perform your duties. Remember your task is to establish credibility and benefit in the *target's* mind!

- Evaluate every aspect or level of your business and social interaction to compile a referral database. Everyone you already know and will meet in the future is a potential source.

- Develop the attitude that you are on duty all the time. A seed planted now may only germinate and grow in the distant future.

- Decide on specific organizational and individual source potential.

- Ensure your ability and comfort level matches your choice. Will a relationship be feasible and mutually productive? Will there be a meeting of like minds?

- Beware of using people or creating the perception of being a *hit and run* merchant - consider every relationship to be a long-term investment.

Sustaining the Relationship

- Develop a reliable follow-up procedure. Ensure access to an efficient data bank facility. Enter all gathered information on a daily basis. Include contact particulars and any follow-up action necessary.

- Be sure to contact the source at the appropriate time, referring to details of the last conversation.

- Commit to a relationship. Sincere, relevant and open interaction is hard work. Your consideration and efforts will lay the foundation to a collaborative and trusting relationship.

- If you are comfortable with an individual, there is no harm in letting it be known that you would appreciate the opportunity to discuss a specific topic. (Suffice it to say, necessary caution should be taken not to *show your hand*.)

- Confidently offer assistance to any perceived requirement; this is an excellent way of establishing your bona fides. Remember, *one good turn begets another!*

- Monitor the referrals and information both given and received. Provide feedback to all concerned, acknowledging the assistance given. A simple *thank you* goes a long way and provides the opportunity for renewed contact with an individual.

- Involve colleagues in intelligence gathering initiatives where possible - create a *ripple effect*. Strange as it may seem, secrecy leads to feelings of exclusion, one of the biggest hindrances to establishing a successful corporate intelligence climate.

Check:

- Are you able to articulate your services/skills/ objective clearly, correctly and concisely?

- Have you exploited all available resources: expertise, reputation, personality, technology, etc.?

For the bold of heart!

- Give people a reason to talk to you - establish yourself as an authority in your field. Volunteer for speaking engagements; and write articles for publication. If you are recognized as a resource, people will ask questions of you and seek your advice.

- Participate in relevant community and charitable activities.

The extent to which these guidelines resonate with you will indicate the extent that you have:

Inspired liking
Inspired respect
Inspired an awareness of/confidence in
your professional expertise

+

Become available for follow up!

Beware the Networking Stampede!

Networking has come to have frightening connotations for anyone who is vaguely *networkable*. The prospect of being *hit on*, for whatever reason, has driven many people who normally enjoy helping others deep underground.

A friend from IBM, for example, refuses nametags at functions and is hugely circumspect before parting with a business card. She explains that event attendance can provoke an unwanted deluge of resumes and calls to discuss potential career paths. Networking pundits advocate aggressive working of the room, exchanging cards with everyone in sight and persistent follow up. The theory is sound, but when embraced by dozens or even hundreds of enthusiastic *networkers* it is time for the most generous of souls to take cover. Imagine receiving twenty entitled or demanding e-mails and telephone calls every time you appear at a business event? It is also sad to see how suspicious people have become of common courtesy - friendliness has, for many, come to mean: "They want something!"

True networking, much like intelligence gathering, relies on the unknown and the chance factor. A friend (A) recently mentioned that he was interested in talking to someone about a specific computer chip development. I had just made the acquaintance with a client (B) who had attended a workshop and in the course of conversation had mentioned a close connection with the cutting edge provider of chips in the US and so was able to facilitate a fruitful meeting.

Consider the factors that went into making the network possible:

- An existing friendship with A that involved mutual respect and trust, allowing a referral to be made with confidence.

- A concerted effort by B to communicate with me beyond the scope of a workshop that inspired liking, respect and a knowledge of the scope of his activity.

- A conscious effort at a later date to remember and connect the worlds of A & B in my own mind.

- The decision to act as facilitator and make the referral; this important step involves risk taking and the effective sale (establishing relevance) of A to B and vice versa.

The Networking Paradox

A relationship is the result of conscious focus. Networking is the disinterested result of relationship interaction:

- Friendship with A and interaction with B were independent and not at all inspired by the desire to network, but rather by the desire to nurture existing relationships.

- The likelihood of A sharing his requirement as well as B informing me of his area of expertise was entirely fortuitous: neither was motivated by any networking goal.

- The agreement by all parties to network was not motivated by any personal gain.

General Relationship Metric

Snapshot Analysis

The chart below clearly shows Alan Jones to be a useful source of reliable information (Rational). He is a straight shooter (Active) with an acutely sensitive (Emotional) streak that causes him to clam up and withdraw (Passive) when he feels that he is being used. Treat him right and he will be collegial and collaborative (Rational).

Alan Jones, IT Consultant, ACME BioTech

Expertise: Information Management Expert, Experienced in Bio Technology fields, Good ability to transfer information, creative/analytical mix; Intellectually generous; Previously employed at AngloTech Inc.

Date of First Contact: 09/12/01

Introduction: Mary Gibbons, Marketing Department
Details forwarded to: Cliff Andrews, IT; Dora Smythe, CI;

Date	Goal	Response				Contact/ Strategy	Result
		Rational (1-10)	Emotional (1-10)	Active (1-10)	Passive (1-10)		
11/21/01	Ask for technical info.	7	2	7	3	Telephone call	✔
11/30/01	Ditto	7	4			Telephone call	✔
12/13/01	Ask for Client lead	6	5	5	5	Telephone call	✔
01/07/02	Enhance relations	6	3	7	4	Lunch	✔
03/06/02	Enhance relations	7	2	7	3	Telephone Call	✔
04/15/02	Ask for industry info.	8	2	7	2	Telephone call	✔

Set and Achieve Your Intelligence Objectives

Dealing with constant change in different societies and communities in various parts of the world has made it impossible for me to believe that fixed rules can prescribe how to handle people or situations. I believe, rather, that guidelines enable effective management of people and situations as they present themselves. The inevitable evolution of life, albeit experienced consciously or sub consciously, impacts on human interaction in unpredictable ways.

In times of great political turbulence with rapidly changing scenarios, I have had to evaluate (at any given moment) people and situations on their particular merits. This soon became an intrinsic way of life. On a personal level, I define love and friendship as the acceptance of people as they are today, not as they were yesterday or how they might be tomorrow. In business, the vicissitudes of the marketplace and the impact of sociopolitical events on the economy make it dangerous to assume certainty. I consider the business world as I find it each day, and plan accordingly. I have learned to deal with *what is* not with *what isn't!*

This approach is called **Point Awareness**™ and describes the subjective and then objective consideration of a situation or person at any point in time. Dynamism and empathy are elements of an understanding that will result in an accurate interpretation of people and events.

Impulse + Question + Subjective & Objective Awareness = Relevant Objective

This might seem like a lot of work, yet people are perfectly capable of deciding what they want and how to get it. They do, however, let go or suspend this inherent human process when inhibited by learned behavior or the unbidden, natural advent of fear. Simply put, when people are fearful, they stop thinking. When they stop thinking, they are unable to make or consider rational choices. The trick is for every individual to find a way to reactivate the thought process when it fails. Point Awareness prevents reliance on a canned, external or prescribed solution.

The thinking process should never be delegated!

Fatigue, Stress, Anger, Ignorance, Insecurity, Poor Self-image, etc. are human conditions that underscore the unknown and potentially give rise to the natural phenomenon we call fear.

In the intelligence world, accepting the unknown or uncertainty as a reality of life is the first step in managing fear, which in turn will ensure continued thinking and (ultimately) rationally secured and evaluated intelligence.

The Indivisibility of the Levels of Being & Point Awareness

Societal and workplace pressures have created a prevailing norm in our society that it is not only highly desirable but also obligatory to keep one's emotional issues to one's self. This is especially true in the workplace. One would be hard pressed to find colleagues who would welcome the intrusion of personal and emotional issues into the work environment.

For practical and bottom line reasons, there may be merit in this view but, in fact, are we talking about something that is remotely possible? Having considered SPICE, how realistic is it to imagine that one can shut off entire levels of existence at a time? Simply put: day by day, whether we like it or not, whatever is happening in our lives will influence how we behave (REAP). This has to be managed if we are to function as human beings. We have been given the innate capacity to think; however, for most of the time the process is subconscious. In times of crisis it needs to be made conscious.

Can it ever be said that we do not think? Conscious thinking will produce an objective that reflects the bigger picture.

S   Unite THINKING and uncertainty

P   Unite THINKING and physical concerns

I   Unite THINKING and learned ability

C   Unite THINKING and interaction with others

E   Unite THINKING and emotions

This process will heighten levels of self and external awareness that are so necessary at any point in the intelligence cycle, ensuring maximum return on energy, resources, and time spent.

Much like a rudder on a ship, Point Awareness provides the focus for full spectrum analysis of people and situational dynamics, and the setting of relevant objectives.

"Cognito ergo sum." ("I think, therefore I am.")

Rene Descartes, Philosopher, Mathematician, and Scientist

Descartes believed that the only thing of which he could be certain was that he existed! He placed emphasis on rationalism, in strong contrast to empiricism, obtaining solutions through deduction and reasoning from the general to the particular.

The Cartesian method, named after him, consists of breaking down every problem into its simplest terms and then building up from the simplest logic to the more complex.

Achieving Point Awareness: *Five Innate Steps to a Realistic Objective*

FACTOR™

A behavioral thermostat to be applied internally and externally:

1. **F**ocus on the person(s)/situation(s). *(What is happening? What is the impulse?)* Subjectively consider all the information at your disposal. Be sure to have accurately identified with whom (or what) you are dealing (SPICE/REAP).

2. **A**ssess the current reality. *(How do I feel about this? How am I reacting?)* Consider how you usually deal with like situations or people; are you satisfied that this is the best approach?

3. **C**reate a positive vision or plan. *(I can see this happening!)* Imagine the desired result. Avoid second guessing. Suspend judgment. Decide to commit to a new vision or *modus operandi* if necessary.

4. **T**est the vision or plan. *(Can this really work? Is it cost effective?)* Does your goal appear to be realistic? Are you ready to commit to the new approach?

5. **O**bjective that is **R**ealistically defined. *(This is what I would like/need to see happen!)* Set your objective: state clearly, correctly and concisely what it is that you are going to achieve.

New information, data, or developments will of necessity dictate a re-evaluation of the desired objective; stay flexible and open to suggestion in order to maintain relevance to the situation or person at hand. Repeat this innate process to check ongoing objective relevance!

Analysts should spend one third of their time traveling to conferences and to study their target, **one third of their time thinking** [...] one third of their time with their customers, seeing what their customers see, understanding their customers problems, and gaining their customers trust [...] to produce superior intelligence on a "just enough, just in time" basis.

Robert David Steele, US Intelligence Veteran

Point Awareness Using FACTOR

Awareness (SPICE) + Thinking (FACTOR) = Efficient Decision Making

Consider the following questions to enhance the FACTOR process of determining how best to respond to changing situations, words, actions and people:

To Reach Point Awareness

- Have I really understood the person or correctly interpreted the situation?

- Have I asked questions or double checked?

- Has one of my hot buttons been pushed?

- Do I have pent up anger/unresolved issues/ baggage in this regard?

- Is this issue a favorite cause of mine?

- How do I usually respond to this sort of thing?

- Do I manage peer group pressure rationally?

- Am I afraid of rejection or being wrong?

- To what extent does this incident typify my behavior?

- Could the person have meant something else?

- How tolerant and flexible am I usually?

- If I am correct in my interpretation, does this incident typify this person?

- What are my choices of response?

- What benefit would each choice bring to me?

- Am I using this incident for an ulterior purpose?

- What would I ideally like to see happen here?

- Have I a game plan to achieve this rationally?

Use **SPICE, REAP & FACTOR** - *expend energy and emotion profitably!* Ask these questions especially when faced with uncertainty, insecurity, anger, fatigue, ignorance, etc.:

- In general interaction with others, have you considered the impact your words or behavior might have?

- Could others possibly interpret you the wrong way?

- What message are you actually conveying?

Lateral Thinking allows for changing concepts and perceptions

With logic you start out with certain ingredients just as in playing chess you start out with given pieces. But what are those pieces? In most real life situations the pieces are not given, we just assume they are there. We assume certain perceptions, certain concepts and certain boundaries. Lateral thinking is concerned not with playing with the existing pieces but with seeking to change those very pieces. Lateral thinking is concerned with the perception part of thinking. This is where we organize the external world into the pieces we can then 'process.'

Edward De Bono

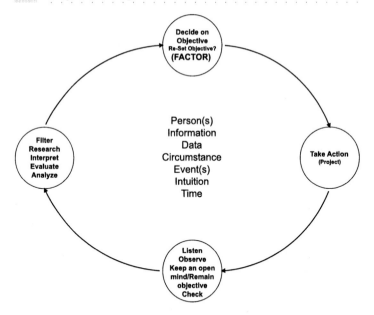

Figure 6.1: The Point Awareness Intelligence Cycle

We are constantly exposed to learning, change, ideas and people. Rationally observe and filter, then absorb, adopt, adapt or discard.

This is an ongoing process without end. Avoid being fixed within the framework of yesterday's dogmas and ideas.

Keeping an Open Mind - Suspending Judgement

In normal day-to-day interaction, we make decisions and arrive at conclusions more often than not by an innate sub-conscious process that will differ from individual to individual, depending on life experience to that point. When there is a lot riding on decision making, consider the benefit of responding rather than reacting to people and situations. Understand your own biases while making important decisions.

- Good intelligence is derived from interpreting the facts, not from making the facts fit the theory!

- Acceptance that the intelligence collection process can only be managed and not controlled is crucial to a successful intelligence operation.

Without contraries there is no progression.

William Blake, *The Marriage of Heaven and Hell*

When you cannot be deceived by men you have realized the wisdom of strategy.

Miyamoto Musashi

Reacting

Impulse/Input

Reaction

Interpretation
Based on perception, instruction, values,
baggage, mistrust

Reaction

Translation
Based on experience/education, religion,
instruction, etc.

Reaction

Action
Based on requirement/incomplete picture, etc.
Potentially inaccurate/wasteful

Responding

Impulse/Input

Check (FACTOR)
Include intuition/gut feelings;
avoid the quest for certainty, etc.

Interpretation

Check (FACTOR)
Ensure flexibility, look further than
existing knowledge/theory

Translation

Check (FACTOR)
Maintain ongoing awareness of developments

Action
Based on real, relevant, accurate, dynamic
information/data

Achieving a Balanced Interpretation of Intelligence

The pressure on the intelligence collector to secure relevant information, make the correct interpretation and forward the right recommendation or report will tempt the most dedicated person to take a short cut at this point. Suspending judgment and allowing possible options to present themselves is very important.

It must be emphasised that there is no right or wrong way of thinking. In the normal course of events, circumstances such as personality, time, resources, budget, emotion/fear, will dictate how the collector will respond or react. The seasoned intelligence worker will be conscious of this difference and evolve a personal system of checks and balances (FACTOR).

The greater the degree that empirical and creative thought modes can co-exist, the greater the chance of securing objective intelligence... subjectively discovered.

Does Creativity Provide the Competitive Edge?

Creativity is about finding, discovery, and making the link between what you've seen and are trying to achieve...you can't find if you're looking - It's a process of osmosis that is dependent on being in a relaxed state of mind...

Creatives need time to stroll and come upon things. We're idea merchants...If you are not fascinated, you simply do not find things ... It's about finding visual stimuli and translating them into stunning creative concepts.

Sean Harrison, Creative Director, Code

Table 6.1: Emprical versus Creative Thinking

Empirical Thinking (Proven)	Creative Thinking (Intuitive/Theoretical)
Prescriptive (one dimensional)	Explores options
Cautious, one frame at a time	Adventurous, logical leaps
Logical progression	Solution, justified retroactively
Looks for certainty, guarantees	Embraces risk/challenge/learning
Ignores change	Adapts to mindset dynamics
Seeks validation from known models and mainstream thought	Embraces the unique, avoids the obvious
Pre-occupation with facts/data/statistics and proof	Comfortable with intuition/gut/chance/the unexplained
Process oriented	Outcome oriented
Single solution	Multi solutions
Accepts	Questions

Intuition Demystified - Factoring in the Unproven!

Intuition describes the instinctive or immediate human response to a person or situation. Whether one believes this response evolves from innate character traits, life experience or the unknown, it is often regarded as an irrational element of the decision-making process as it is not rooted in proven factual context.

It is suggested that intuition is very much a real part of human existence and interaction and is at work whether we like it or not. Understanding intuition is important as it closely parallels the intelligence-gathering process. Clues are provided without context or empirical proof.

The danger of ignoring the existence of clues (intuition) is very real. Decisions made without regard for subjective perceptions in an individual, team, departmental and corporate context will often result in the failure to gather relevant information, reach informed conclusions and make decisions that reflect or shape the culture of an organization.

Intuition is like receiving a message from an unknown source. Broadly speaking, that source is known as the subconscious. To build familiarity and trust with this undeniable part of the human make up, consider the following steps:

- Recognize the subconscious as a potential source of inspiration or solutions. Build on small everyday occurrences where you receive a mysterious helping hand. (E.g. finding car keys, where you parked your car, etc.) If trust becomes an element in these small incidents, would it not be reasonable to open up to the possibility of larger or more significant assistance?

- In daily interaction with others, set clear objectives and ask the subconscious for assistance.

- Let go! Wait for the answer to come to you. As discussed earlier, the quest for certainty is an exercise in control. Your mind is in search mode and the answers will come to you.

The process of ***making conscious what is innate*** requires trusting the unexplained and will be difficult if it requires building trust from scratch.

To Consider

Just as a computer has hidden files, cookies, meta tags, temporary files, etc. so the human brain has the capacity to search, filter and analyze its own database while consciously engaged in other activity. Just as the computer contains a large amount of unused or underutilized functions, the human capacity for research and solution providing may remain untapped. Circumstance may provide an adrenaline rush that will necessitate blind reliance on intuition. Consider the advantage of being able to confidently and **consciously** engage this resource.

Intuition and the Innovative Thought Dynamic

The experienced intelligence worker, comfortable and confident with usual process, proven strategy and familiar relationships, will inadvertently allow the known to override the unknown – conveniently fitting new developments, situations or people into the parameters of past experience. In the intelligence world, intuition is often the only *alarm* a person will receive that will prompt a rethink of an objective, plan, strategy or procedure.

FACTOR should be consciously deployed when intuitive feelings arise.

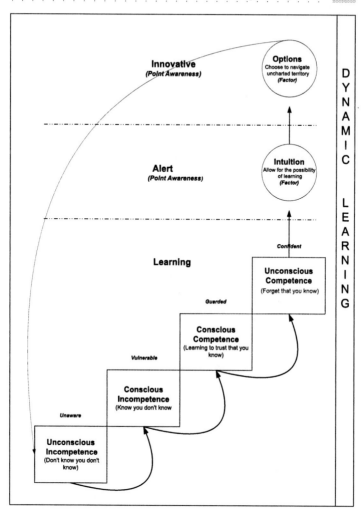

Figure 6.2: The Learning Curve + Innate Intuition + Action = Dynamic Intelligence Potential

Intuition Refused ... A Warning

Simply put, intuition involves nothing more than listening to a hunch. Listening to a hunch involves walking an unknown path. An unknown path does not have a known end point. Intuition has not yet happened; it is an immeasurable, an intangible concept that together with a potential affect will only be verifiable at some point in the future!

For those who limit themselves to the tried and tested (the proven and the safe) intuition will more often than not be suppressed or dismissed as nonsense or as *touchy feely* stuff that has no place in business. The net effect of protracted refusal to admit the value of a hunch on organizational culture will be

- Limited innovation - ideas will be accepted only if they fit known parameters. People talking of innovation will generally mean downloading or recycling something that that has worked elsewhere.

- Intelligence, information or ideas will not be shared unless there is a guarantee of 100% accuracy.

- Solutions provided internally or externally will be driven by a given hypothesis: business circumstances will be made to fit a prescribed template (what worked for X will work for you, or I want to have what worked for X).

- The team *role* of intelligence gatherer will disappear. Big picture thinking will slowly diminish, and individuals will ensure that only their immediate responsibilities are accounted for.

- The general organizational culture will become risk averse.

- The organization will ultimately stagnate.

The Tapping

Bushmen refer to *tapping* within themselves - a physical manifestation of a profound gift for intuitive apprehension of the future ... Only a fool would go on ignoring his tapping...if he does not sit and listen to his tapping it could utterly leave him.

Laurens van der Post, *A Far-Off Place*

Strategy & Intuition - The Known vs. The Unknown

One of the biggest challenges in strategizing to evolve a workable analysis from gathered intelligence is a reluctance to deal with foreknowledge: what *might* happen, as opposed to what *will* happen. Certainty and the quest for ultimate control seem a more ready objective for most than that of managing the unknown.

To manage this resistance, set an objective to create awareness of what it is that will ensure organizational survival in today's business world. Companies that succeed have underlying cultures that demonstrate

- Courage to manage the unknown - factoring in uncertainty and recognizing that control is elusive

- Preparedness to work with what is, and not what should be - embracing contraries, confrontation, debate, etc. as opportunities for progression

- Energy to treat every situation, person, and day as a new experience, making no assumptions

- Acceptance of the concepts of risk, delegation, assistance, trust, and flexibility

- Willingness to make choices based on all experiences to date - understanding gut feelings and intuition

- The ability to pursue variables, make choices and embrace visions that are not deemed current, usual, or appropriate

Listening to a Hunch!

We can talk *ad nauseam* about intuition, flexibility, leadership, individuality and creativity. Only with an understanding of them as the unknown within the framework of the known, however, will we come to consider them as concepts that underpin the business world.

The CEO of a hugely successful Canadian gold mining company once described how a hunch had saved his organization from a disastrous merger. Contract finalizations had been ongoing for over a year, building on due diligence that predated the initial agreement. His team had worked long and hard to arrive at the point of final signature, yet on the eve of the event he called his accountant and lawyer late at night, informing them that the deal was off. Just on a hunch… there was no way he could logically substantiate his decision or put his finger on what it was that had spooked him!

Naturally, his team thought he had flipped out yet within weeks, the wisdom of his decision became apparent. As it transpired, the prospective partner organization had several well-hidden skeletons in its closet. The merger might well have been a catastrophic business move.

Would it not be logical to assume that if organizational leaders collectively accepted the unknown as an ever present factor in business that a bigger picture approach to strategy and planning would follow?

The Bigger Picture: Intelligence & Value Diversity

The intelligence trail will often necessitate delving into history and making sense of what people did or omitted to do in bygone years. Today, efficient filing/database systems, easy access to information, and the Internet make this an increasingly easy task with profound benefit. Modern technology and scientific advances often enable us to interpret the past with stunning accuracy.

It is important to remember, however, that in as much as the world of science has changed, so have customs, values and societal norms. Carefully consider SPICE and FACTOR when researching people and situations from a different era or even decade.

Documentary Inaccuracies

It is interesting to see how often modern investigative journalists and biographers accuse yesterday's personalities of being less than honest - their conclusions being sparked by date and age discrepancies on official documentation such as wedding certificates, job and passport applications, etc. The stigma that attached to poverty, adoption, divorce, illegitimacy, ethnicity/religion, age, sexual orientation, etc. was very real (and still is in some circles) for most of the 20th century. Unhappily, people who had *made it* or wanted to *make it* in society or business were obliged to take great pains to conceal their origins and other skeletons that lurked in their closets. It is very unfair and dangerous from an intelligence viewpoint to judge them according to the more relaxed social mores we enjoy today. Posturing, and getting away with it, was an accepted part of life in business and high society circles. The latter is almost impossible today given the ever-

vigilant media and the speedy, efficient communication
and surveillance systems at their disposal.

Care should be taken to view perceived
documentary inaccuracies with circumspection. Assume
nothing - think big!

Lack of Documentary Proof

People born after 1970 find it hard to believe that a paper
trail can be non existent. In the pre-computer era, fires,
inefficiency and carelessness often resulted in
documentary inconsistencies, irregularities or the loss of
vital records that were never rectified or replaced. One
such consequence was that people often had to estimate
key dates, their age, or that of their children or parents.

Espirit de Corps of the Intelligence World

The *intelligence profile* clearly requires a low desire for
recognition and fanfare. Dedicated intelligence workers
have a strong service orientation and deep sense of
commitment to their employer, industry or nation.

The ethical code of silence means a great deal to
these people. Many former intelligence workers will
remain committed to silence as they believe that even the
passage of time would not take away the embarrassment,
consequence and potential sense of betrayal felt by people
involved in their covert activities.

Oftentimes, huge chunks of history are purposely
not recorded and indeed false records are sometimes kept
to deter prying minds. Many a good analyst or historian
has difficulty reconciling conflicting verbal and written
versions of events. For example, consider post-World War
II chronicles that abound with inaccuracies due to varying
priorities and records emanating from Military, Foreign

Office and Intelligence circles. Some people remain tight-lipped, others do not. Some embellish, while others underplay the truth. The analyst is at times sorely tempted to go with the most eloquent version.

"… the best thing I could do was shut up …"

Benjamin De Forest (Pat) Bayly, the largely unknown Canadian hero of WWII whose brilliant encryption/decryption work saved countless lives and gave the Allies an unquestioned competitive edge, maintained the point of view that he should never be known by name. He refused to write up an account of his secret intelligence activities after the war saying:

"I wasn't having any of that, because I had been treated extremely well by Canada, the States and England - far beyond what was necessary. I was welcomed into places where it was absolutely necessary that I be … and everybody's been so very kind. … We'd go out and have a couple of drinks and they'd tell me political things that shouldn't be free, … they were really quite outspoken and I came to the conclusion at the end of the war that the best thing I could do was shut up. Because if I did, if I spoke all the things I would unwittingly mention, things would have political (consequences)…."

Quoted in *The True Intrepid* by Bill Macdonald (RAINCOAST Books)

The *Need to Know*

As with most intelligence institutions, businesses are notorious for denying the very existence of their intelligence gathering operations and agents. In the event of an intelligence operation failure or exposure, very little in the way of support or accountability can be expected from an employer. Knowledge of an intelligence objective and operation will more likely than not be restricted to those who need to know.

The age-old maxim "Do not let the left hand know what the right is doing" is very much the rule of thumb in many traditional intelligence circles.

Forensic journalism conducted years later can produce what looks like clear evidence to support a certain theory. For example, a retired CFO claims to have "monitored every dollar that came in or left the company and for sure Mr. X was not on the payroll and operation Y did not take place." This person might be telling the truth; however, only with the facts at his or her disposal.

Intelligence Objectives: Asking for Assistance

In the age of hype, disinformation, spin-doctors and international media manipulation, the decision maker cannot afford to make knee-jerk assumptions. The ability to respond responsibly to challenge and ever changing sociopolitical and industrial scenarios is too great a burden for a single individual to bear. Assistance should always be at hand.

Technology

Caught between the need for quick action and accurate intelligence assessment, a good array of tools will come in handy. Integration, Competitive Intelligence, Knowledge Management and CRM software and familiarity with the Internet will allow for quick verification of trends and interpretations made from processed intelligence products. Remember that these tools are only as current as the input received or as good as the person who uses them.

The Internet as a medium for the sharing of information is indisputably held to be *the* indispensable tool for intelligence sharing in years to come.

Trusted Advisors / Relationships

In the section on relationship building, the necessity of having trusted individuals in the industry, able and willing to provide intelligence was heavily underscored. So too when verifying information - the ease or facility with which a trusted advisor, client, contact or friend can be relied on to confirm thoughts or the need for policies or an approach will make all the difference when ambiguity and confusion occur.

The Cliché: Self-Doubt - Manipulation (The Hamster Syndrome)

The cliché is an ever increasing and nauseating part of our reality! A repeated idea on CNN or other mass media vehicles often brings the phrase/concept to collective consciousness in hours. It becomes almost *de rigueur* to quote such phrases as a prelude to every written or spoken presentation: "Now that the world has changed forever..." "He electrified the nation..." "The collapse of the dot.com empire..." "The Internet heyday", "Weapons of Mass Destruction", "Roadmap to Peace", "Collateral Damage" to name a few... Repetition will validate a single opinion, mediocre policies or create a factually erroneous perception in the minds of non-thinkers.

While this phenomenon may be irritating in daily life, it is catastrophic in the world of intelligence gathering. It requires a conscious decision to say "I do not agree. This is, for me, untrue and my reasons are as follows..." **Failure to risk herd disapproval will result in tired and second-hand intelligence.**

Intelligence gathering is not about popularity, but rather a quest for survival in a fiercely competitive and cutthroat world. Our hitherto privileged circumstances should not blind us to the danger of existing (unconscious) as opposed to living (conscious) in a precarious world.

The Hamster Syndrome™

Although nice enough in their natural habitat, nothing can be more evocative of futility than the sight of a caged hamster valiantly burning energy on a treadmill with no apparent objective. Does it make sense to expend a great amount of effort without a result of equal proportion? Are we ever *hamster-like* in our decision making? There are many references to the hamster syndrome made every day. Some include *peer-group pressure, knee-jerk reaction, inference, keeping up with the Jones', sheep, lemmings*, etc.

The Theory

An impulse/input/action is received, positive or negative, from an individual (10% of the population will generate impulses at any point in time). For the sake of peace, lack of self-esteem, confidence or even apathy, we often let things pass unchallenged or go along with people without thinking why we do what we do. (20% of the population will react in this manner at any point in time.) This is a dangerous state of affairs as the average person (70% of the population at any point in time) believing in the greater good of the human race will tend to believe that this group (20%) is acting in a rational and purposeful manner. In other words 10% are appeased by 20% who are followed in good faith by 70%. Every individual at one time or another will fit into one of these categories. When in the 20% group, the individual will unconsciously decide not to think and is in *Hamster Mode*! (This unscientifically tested theory is based solely on the personal observations of the author.)

The full impact of non-thinking can be well illustrated by the general population in Germany in the 1930s. Although Adolph Hitler was initially considered a joke by most, he promised certainty to a fearful and consequently unthinking people, suffering under the post WWI reparation deal laid out by the Treaty of Versailles. His aggressive politics and the threatening tactics of his henchmen (10%) cowed or attracted those in the immediate vicinity (20%), leading the population at large (70%) to assume that "this fellow must have something, so many appear to validate him…" They unthinkingly followed.

How often has this phenomenon been seen in recent times on the world stage, in our national/provincial/municipal affairs and even in our homes? In business, the Hamster Syndrome, in addition to making us vulnerable to the machinations of competitors, is a block to innovation and originality.

Independent Thought

The need for validation from others is natural, even necessary, but danger lurks if this becomes a sub conscious goal. Question everything, situation by situation, arriving at well thought out conclusions. Can you afford complacency or one-dimensional reactions to events and their origin? Say what you mean, and mean what you say … and be prepared to pay the price. You have this right!

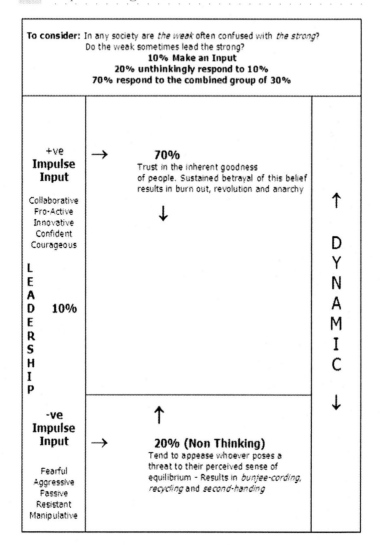

To consider: In any society are *the weak* often confused with *the strong*?
Do the weak sometimes lead the strong?
10% Make an Input
20% unthinkingly respond to 10%
70% respond to the combined group of 30%

+ve
Impulse
Input

Collaborative
Pro-Active
Innovative
Confident
Courageous

L
E
A
D **10%**
E
R
S
H
I
P

-ve
Impulse
Input

Fearful
Aggressive
Passive
Resistant
Manipulative

→ **70%**
Trust in the inherent goodness
of people. Sustained betrayal of this belief
results in burn out, revolution and anarchy
↓

↑
20% (Non Thinking)
Tend to appease whoever poses a
threat to their perceived sense of
equilibrium - Results in *bunjee-cording,*
recycling and *second-handing*

↑
D
Y
N
A
M
I
C
↓

Figure 6.3: This model is intended only as a partial interpretation of a single aspect of human interaction.

In the world of intelligence, consider the peril involved when a hamster in disguise, the ***bunjee-corder*** (Active/Passive/Emotional) who is awash with energy, dominates an operation or project. This individual will engage in drama, promise action and results, and then beat a carefully camouflaged retreat! Theories are talked up and down, people are shuffled to and fro and tactics discussed while the hidden objective is merely to avoid rocking the boat. The appropriate effort is apparent for all to see, but the action is not designed to produce a tangible result. It can be termed a safe experience (Passive) but it is only when the music suddenly stops that we see *the emperor has no clothes.*

Similarly **recyclers** (Active/Passive) with copycat theories, tactics, and policies that *secondhand* the success of previous innovators will have a catastrophic effect on the relevance of intelligence produced. Every employee has a wealth of new information and experience that is of potential use to the organization.

When faced with *recyclers* and *bunjee-corders,* or even the possibility of being one, we need to take a moment to determine an appropriate objective:

- "What do I want to see happen?"

- "Have I made a positive contribution?"

- "Have I bottled good ideas because I am scared of rejection?

- "Am I looking for certainty?

- "Am I conforming to a corporate or societal template?"

Leadership which is evil, while it may temporarily succeed, always carries within itself the seeds of its own destruction.

- Montgomery of Alamein

Table 6.2: The Perils of Corporate Non-Thinking

Lack of unique corporate/product identity

Outdated product and service

Stifled individuality and originality = Poor/No advance Planning

Inadequate contingency planning - vulnerability to sudden market swings and changes in traditional patterns

Vulnerability to manipulation internally/externally

High risk of a loss of stock holder confidence

Inefficient use of technology

Unnecessary expenditure on ineffective technology and consulting services

Lip service to employee training and career planning

A staid, lack-luster work force

Stagnation and lack of growth

Organizational Fatigue

Is preoccupation with tried and tested process and formulaic solutions ringing the death knell for innovation and originality in the world of information and knowledge management?

To an alarming extent, the corporate world is faced with clients who want duplication of something seen elsewhere. Given that *the client is always right*, are information gatherers becoming cut-and-paste solution providers, laying down the recognizable and only the tried and tested for as many clients as possible? Has *recycling* become the dominant trend? How sustainable is this trend in any industry? To what extent is important intelligence watered down to neutral viewpoints and safe policy recommendations?

The corporate culture that stifles potentially discordant intelligence input is in real danger of relying on stale information. The tendency to do or say what is expected, safe or proven when collecting and processing intelligence will result in organizational stagnation.

To ensure that healthy thinking will allow for effective analysis of information, data and events on a daily basis, use all technology and industry resources available. The personal opinion and interpretation an employee brings to the application and use of products such as tracking software, database applications, computer profiling applications, etc. will establish the real value of the technology. Remember that these products are provided to a multitude of clients, all who believe they have the cutting edge technology that will put them ahead in business.

Every individual at one time or another will consciously decide not to think. The trick is to encourage the assumption of responsibility when important issues are at stake. Corporate Intelligence Awareness will make it difficult for a loyal employee to ignore the opportunity to contribute to the effective operation of the organization.

To Consider

"A society which emphasizes uniformity is one which creates intolerance and hate. A society which eulogizes the average citizen is one which breeds mediocrity."

- Pierre E. Trudeau

Put in positive terms:

Create a tolerant and innovative operational environment. Encourage and accept individuality within the framework of corporate objectives. Your organization will have an in-built and accessible resource of innovation equipped to navigate difficulty in the face of uncertainty.

Hamster Mode - Self Testing

On a scale of 1 (rarely) to 5 (often), please indicate with a circle the degree to which you feel the following statements best reflect your approach to people and situations:

You prefer your doctor to give you MRI and lab results rather than a personal opinion.
1   2   3   4   5

You would think twice before seeing a film that had received a lousy review.
1   2   3   4   5

A colleague or your boss makes consistently erroneous statements in meetings. You consider it inappropriate to challenge him or her.
1   2   3   4   5

For you, CNN gives the best all round news coverage in the world.
1   2   3   4   5

You rarely notice people saying one thing but actually meaning another.
1   2   3   4   5

Even though you know the car is not running well, you accept the service station report that their diagnostic centre (machine) cannot find anything wrong.
1   2   3   4   5

When expressing dissatisfaction as a customer, you feel better when given an overview of the company's standard procedure.

1   2   3   4   5

People admire your easy going nature, yet you feel like a door mat.

1   2   3   4   5

You are known for firm right/left wing political views.

1   2   3   4   5

Others achieve recognition for things you thought of, but did not act upon.

1   2   3   4   5

Scoring

40-50: Make a conscious effort to deliver a more positive contribution. Do not let others always decide what is best for you.

30-40: Take more calculated risks. Accept the unknown as a given in your life. Love your neighbor *as* not better than yourself!

20-30: Keep the fine balance of subjectivity/objectivity in your consciousness. Use FACTOR and SPICE.

Fear & the Abdication of Decision-Making Responsibility

Is it possible that someone could agree to or participate in a course of action that would be potentially harmful to an organization in total contradiction of personal knowledge and beliefs simply because of an inability to speak up? I believe that recognition of this common and frightening reality in the business world will be an important first step in fighting this tendency.

As stated previously, setting primary goals that demand certainty is the same as asking for the impossible. An organization with consistently rigid goals, impossible deadlines, extreme political correctness and a host of zero tolerance workplace regulations would be indicative of an *absolute* environment. The degree to which this organizational culture is enforced will result in a corresponding climate of *fear*.

Table 6.3: How a Climate of Fear Leads to Stifled Decision-Making	
Corporate Absolutism	*Possible Effects of Fear*
Top-down hierarchy (Boss is always right)	"Yes man" response; avoidance of any form of risk/failure; stifling of initiative/creativity; dishonest reports back; sabotage; deceit; sidestepping the possibility of disapproval, rejection, or ridicule; a compliant, servile team

Inflexible/unrealistic targets	Burn out; manipulation of reality; dishonesty; corruption; falsified documentation; erosion of best practice ethics
Impossible deadlines	Short cuts; unverified work; template-solutions; stereotypical reports; lack of originality
Job specific function (strict application)	Compartmentalized approach to work; no extra input; erosion of enthusiasm/loyalty; rumors/gossip
Zero tolerance & excessive political correctness in the operational culture	Hypocrisy, passive aggression, rumor mongering; deceit; stifling of open communication; preoccupation with form rather than substance; ultimate stagnation
Fear = Irrationality/Non Thinking = Stifled Decision-Making	

Examples of *Disruption by Fear*

Scenario 1

Company:

IT Solutions Inc. (fictitious)

Mission:

Provide comprehensive information system solutions

Culture:

Highly compartmentalized operational model; strict adherence to job description and departmental function

Intelligence & Events:

- Head Technical Coder reports to VP operations (rational) that she has an acquaintance in an international consulting company. It would appear that they are looking to engage competent IT solution providers. She is told: "We have our marketing and sales people pretty much on top of things. We cannot have the whole company running in with suggestions ... we'd be here all day!" (active/passive)

- The next attempt to the sales director is met with: "Thanks but we prefer to engage agencies only to use our services .... So much easier..." (active)

Intelligence Blockage & Possible Devolution:

- The team member feels silly/angry/rejected and will certainly think twice before offering intelligence again… (emotional/passive)

- Spreads the word internally/externally that sending information upward is a waste of time, thereby discouraging others from reporting industry intelligence/leads… (emotional/active)

- Begins moonlighting for the contact at the consulting company. A deal is struck and several key players leave the company to start their own business. This event represents a blow with regard to industry reputation as well as a huge financial loss represented by investment in technical training of the individuals over the last year

- News of resignations leads to loss of one existing and two new accounts to the direct competitor

Competitive Advantage lost

- Blocking the internal intelligence process in its own turn became intelligence for the competition and potential clients

- Lack of basic human acknowledgement and failure to encourage/absorb big picture thinking resulted in:

  - Financial loss

  - Employee resignation

  - Damage to corporate reputation

Scenario 2

Company:

National Water Works (fictitious, parastatal)

Mission:

Provide clean drinking water province wide

Culture:

Top down hierarchy. Input not encouraged; remote, ineffective supervision; poor hiring practices

Actual Government:

Autocratic; self righteous; dogmatic (active)

Intelligence & Events:

- Sporadic illnesses in children and the elderly that appear e-coli related

- Increase in reported illnesses

- Medical reports suggest drinking water as a possible source

- Individual company members take initiative and draw conclusions that perhaps the water sources are contaminated and ask for guidance (rational).

- Supervisors (active) slap down input as "Rumors… We have the safest drinking water in the world…" The government has several crisis issues on at the time and similarly denies the

possibility, citing a proud record of safety"
(active/passive).

- Individuals long used to this behavior realize the
futility of pushing and decide to back off in a
"why should we care" manner (passive).

Intelligence Blockage & Possible Devolution:

- The increased illnesses go unreported (passive).

- They become sporadic deaths that prompt a full
scale inquiry that uncovers unsafe drinking water
in several locations.

Why would individuals whose job it is to safeguard
drinking water ignore proof that something was amiss?

Competitive Advantage lost

- Inertia and organizational fatigue prevented
individuals (passive) from pressuring management
to respond to their belief that the water was
polluted.

- Timely interpretation of the realities facing the
company would have enabled action to be taken
to remedy the situation:

  - In the prevention of deaths

  - Saving the company reputation

This scenario is based on a true series of events where
individuals consciously acted in the worst interests of
themselves, their organization and their community.

Scenario 3

Company:

Super Genomics Ltd. (fictitious)

Mission:

Stem cell and related medical development research

Culture:

Secretive; founding partners both highly motivated and competitive; long history of *one-upsmanship;* Sam (junior) is continually put down by Tom (senior) who is a real *know-it-all.*

Intelligence & Events:

- Sam is plugged into the industry network; he hears that a genomics company has opened and is pursuing identical research to their own.

- Sam becomes convinced as additional intelligence becomes available that the company's security has been compromised. The competitor has, he believes, direct insight into the inner and secret research of the company.

- Tom (emotional/active) dismisses his theories on both occasions.

- Sam decides to hang the senior partner *out to dry* (emotional/passive) and does nothing further to warn Tom of the many developments taking place.

- Within a period of twelve months, Sam is proved correct: the competitor goes to market with a patented version of their still to be marketed product.

- They file for bankruptcy, unable financially to continue with new research or to prove their case against the competitor.

How is it possible that Sam could not have acted in a more forceful way?

Intelligence Blockage & Possible Devolution:

- The intelligence flow remained intact throughout the process.

- The corporate pathology and related emotional issues proved to be a stronger stimulus than corporate survival.

Competitive Advantage lost

Purposeful persuasion would have enabled:

- The information leak to be plugged

- Timely action to alter the course of research

This scenario is based on a real life circumstance.

Scenario 4

Company:

RichMan Mutual Funds (fictitious)

Mission:

Investment fund sales and management

Culture:

Politically correct; makes strong case for collaborative work environment; confrontation not encouraged;

Intelligence & Events:

- The CFO, Paul, brings intelligence to a top-level meeting showing projected growth strategies of the competition.

- Allan, one of the team members, recognizes the information as part of an exercise the competitor was recently involved in. It bears no relation whatsoever to reality.

- He says nothing as RichMan strongly discourages contact with the competition. His involvement with a woman who works there is how he knows about the exercise; to reveal this fact would potentially compromise his good standing in the CFO's eyes. He knows from previous experience that to prove (the obviously triumphant) Paul wrong at this meeting would have serious personal repercussions in the future.

- RichMan hires consultants to evaluate the strategy and embarks on a campaign to meet the challenges of the competitor's plan.

Intelligence Blockage & Possible Devolution:

- Paul and the company (active/passive) give lip service to a collaborative corporate culture.

- Allan is paralyzed by fear (emotional/passive).

How is it possible that Allan can sit by and watch as the company goes so hopelessly down the wrong path?

Competitive Advantage lost

If Allan had spoken up he would have:

- Completed the intelligence circuit with regards to the competitor

- Saved the company thousands of wasted dollars in consultants fees and time

- Avoided putting the company and his own financial well being in jeopardy

This scenario is based on real life circumstance in an unrelated industry.

Strategic Intelligence Delivery

At some time or other, everyone experiences the frustration of saying something very simple and at a later point realizing that a person has understood something completely different. Conversely, it is equally stupefying when someone says they said or did not say something that we would swear was entirely clear and unambiguous. It is also often difficult to comprehend the level of resistance present when unwelcome intelligence is put forward, even though it is clearly in the best interests of the organization.

Familiarity with corporate hierarchy and a degree of comfort with the way things are done in any organization will always be recognizable cause for resistance should someone rock the boat. Given that intelligence (of its very nature) will demand change or warn of impending doom and that, as we have seen, individuals across the corporate spectrum have the potential to act irrationally when faced with threatening situations, it is advisable to assume that *all* intelligence has to be *sold* internally.

Wisdom vs. Power

The *seller* has the task of persuading the relevant persons that the intelligence has consequence for the organization. It would be helpful to factor into the equation the following permanent cautions regarding the *buyer*:

- There will be a natural resistance to any element that threatens the status quo, especially if it threatens his or her power base.

- The buyer is not aware until the moment of presentation of all the facts at the seller's disposal and may be shocked by the seller's revelations.

- There is a possibility that the buyer will not be in a position to fully focus on the issue at the time of the attempted sale.

As evidenced by SPICE, REAP, and FACTOR, **Point Awareness**™ will illustrate the potential complexity of the intelligence sale (buyer and seller) at any point in time and the resultant inability to guarantee that a particular

---

Questions provide an effective *thermostat* function that give an immediate indication of the success of every step of the communication process. They serve to acknowledge and draw others into a thinking or Rational State (REAP).

message has been heard and understood. Simply put, the seller has the task of persuading a potentially reluctant buyer to think clearly and act quickly. Time and effort spent in this regard is worth the investment.

If every communication is treated as a sale, this effective communication will soon become second nature:

- This is what is on offer. (Objective/offer)

- This is why you need to buy. (Relevance/benefit)

- This is the process. (Detail)

- Will you buy/Do you want it? (Close)

- What has changed since your decision was made? (Follow up)

Direct vs Indirect Communication

Speaking directly means saying what you mean and
meaning what you say. To effectively process intelligence
internally, time is of the essence. Care must be taken to
speak as clearly and directly as possible to ensure that the
intelligence and its relevance to the organization is
understood. It is in everyone's best interest if the
corporate culture embraces open discussion and does not
become sidetracked by irrelevant issues. It is suggested
that challenge, argument, and confrontation are elements
that are essential if the intelligence is to be analysed,
evaluated and adopted.

People react differently to any communication.
Good intelligence will (of necessity) indicate a potential
change in the status quo and may involve protracted
debate on certain levels. Face issues squarely to arrive at a
firmly agreed evaluation of the new intelligence, its
relevance, and the possible options for its absorption into
the decision making process:

- Do not confuse diplomacy and tact with indirect
  or ulterior talk.

- Do not confuse directness with aggression and
  rudeness.

- Do not confuse debate or negotiation with
  resistance.

- Do not confuse confrontation with conflict.

Table 7.1: How People React to New Intelligence is Dependent upon their Emotional State

State (REAP)	Potential Reaction to New Intelligence
Rational	Listen; ask questions to clarify; debate; make recommendations
Active	Dismiss, override or ridicule; Draw Us VS Them battle lines
Emotional	Go of on a tangent/ bog the proceedings down with unrelated issues; Criticize/blame others up front
Passive	Ignore, negate or find excuses to avoid confrontation; Criticize/blame others behind their backs

Five Rules for Effective Communication (FERMA)

1. Formulate and state a realistic objective (FACTOR)

This is what I want; am I clear?

State your objective. The analyst needs to know exactly what you want to see happen or have to offer. This step saves time and reflects basic courtesy.

2. Establish relevance or consequence to the analyst

Do you see why you should listen to me?

Ensure that you establish awareness in all concerned as to why your objective is necessary. Secure involvement. Do not presume that the analyst has understood. To inform is to acknowledge!

3. Rational behavior inspires rational response

Do you understand the process and requirements? What are your concerns?

Listen, observe and interpret. Your words and actions should be collaborative at all times. Questions are extremely effective in promoting dialogue and stemming the flow of irrational behavior. Relevant questions should reflect an awareness of the person and situation at hand and will usually result in a thought-out response. Communication is a two way street: measure your progress by the response received.

4. **Make others take responsibility for their words and actions by asking questions that establish ownership**

    Will you do it? Am I correct in assuming that you agree?

    These questions will allow you to measure the success of your communication. Positive responses indicate that you have established an understanding or acceptance of your objective. In conflict situations, adversaries are obliged to explain their behavior.

5. **Always hold on to secured objectives**

    May I ask why you did not do it? What did you mean by...?

    Should further transactions in the pursuit of your objective be necessary, the secured objective serves as the point of first reference and obviates the need to go over ground already gained!

Human Context & the Sale of Intelligence

There are two paradoxical schools of thought regarding the internal sale and evaluation of intelligence.

Logically, the more one knows about how, whence and from whom the intelligence was procured, the easier it will be to prioritize and make an eventual decision as to the value of the information received. On the other hand, this knowledge might color or create bias in the mind of a potential intelligence client.

It is true, although often difficult to believe, that many in the business world make costly decisions based purely on emotional responses to people, situations, and circumstances against a backdrop of previous positive or negative experience. In my opinion, no amount of politically correct posturing will undo this fact.

Beware!

Context, interpretation, and prediction are intangible and dynamic human activities resulting in provoked emotions that either allow or disallow the easy sale of relevant intelligence. This situation again highlights the fact that there are no set rules in the world of selling or purchasing intelligence. For this reason I have continually stressed the importance of individual capacity to

- Maintain an awareness of the bigger picture. (Point Awareness)

- Set rational objectives in a dynamic environment (FACTOR)

- Understand behavioral responses in **themselves** and **others** (REAP)

- Deliver an accurate message that establishes immediate relevance (FERMA)

- Maintain healthy, trusting relationships

Fact/Information + Context + Interpretation/Prediction = Intelligence

I made it my business to get to know all the commanders and their staffs personally. This was a very special sort of intelligence and required a special relationship if the best was to be got out of Ultra. I did not share the view…that all intelligence must be impersonal and under no circumstances must there be any contact or acknowledgement of the source by the commander. Ultra's broad coverage provided those who continually handled it with a large amount of background information, in addition to that culled from reading so many of the signals of the German High Command; I found it was this that the majority of commanders were always interested to know about.

F.W. Winterbotham, 'The Ultra Spy'

Author's Note: The Ultra Network was created to disseminate the decoded German secret messages to Allied frontline commanders as quickly as possible. Placing the message in Allied context as well as providing the background to its procurement made for effective decision making. Despite this fact many commanders, in their wisdom, saw fit to ignore much of the context in view of their own ambitions or emotional responses, often with disastrous results.

Editor's Note: To find out more about how Winston Churchill used the intelligence gained from Ultra to change the course of WWII, read *Churchill's Adaptive Enterprise: Lessons for Business Today.* Details on this title are at the back of this book.

Making Content Work

Speak/Write in Sound Bites

A sound bite is a short unambiguous group of words that illustrates a concept. Politicians faced with radio microphones and television cameras make full use of the 15-30 seconds, the average length of time allocated by the media to any single speaker on daily news programs. They cannot afford to say anything that can be edited, quoted out of context or used to make them look stupid! The sound bite is a useful technique to use in oral or written communication.

In the realm of corporate intelligence communication, speaking in sound bites saves time, leaves no room for confusion and allows for easy preparation for presentations, interviews, and stressful meetings. Persuasion of others as to the relevance of a particular message is key to the justification or validation of hard work. Failure to persuade or sell a specific item of intelligence negates the effort, time and cost of the collection process. The art of unambiguous speaking and writing requires practice.

Clear, Correct & Concise Language

- Practice thinking in sound bites by describing people, things, and situations in three words.

- Ask internally if the three words accurately express the thought that inspired them.

- Develop the three words into a concept.

- Express the concept in a phrase, a sentence, a paragraph.

- Choose the appropriate time for words, phrases, sentences or paragraphs. Work on a *need to know* basis.

- Say what you mean, mean what you say!

To Consider:

Opening *Windows Explorer* reveals the computer's drives;

Click on a drive, the directories appear;

Click on a directory, the sub-directories appear…

When using a specific computer for the very first time, would it make sense to open a sub-directory or even a directory first?

Sound Bites in Action

From a comparison of the following scenarios, consider the value of the sound bite:

1ˢᵗ Communication Scenario between A & B: (Consider written, electronic or verbal media)

A - I would like to meet with you sometime.
B - OK.

A - Could I talk to you about business?
B - Sure.

A - When could we meet?
B - Anytime.

A - Could I meet you Wednesday?
B - Sounds good. What time?

A - I was thinking breakfast
B - I can't do that. I take the kids to school.

A - How about lunch?
B - Fine!

A - Where would you like to meet?
B - Jake's Fish Grill. OK with you?

A - No can do - I am allergic to fish.
B - Italian OK? Alfredo's?

A - Great! I am looking forward to talking to you about bio-genomic trends.
B - Bio-genomic trends?

A - Yeah!
B - Sorry, I'm in pharmaceuticals - sales, actually.

2nd Scenario: (Communication in sound bite form)

A - I would like your insights on bio-genomic trends. Could we meet for lunch soon?
B - It would be great to get together, but I am in the Pharmaceutical field, not bio-genomics.

If the answer was 'yes,'

A - Would you choose the time and place? I eat anything except fish.

Be clear, correct, and concise! Consider the time saved; this is especially relevant in more complicated, crucial or stressful circumstances.

Bridging the Communication & Cultural Divide

Advanced communication networks, information technology, travel and migration patterns have made diversity a part of every day life. The myriad of languages, customs, value-systems, etc. that make up the world we live in make it impossible to learn every nuance of every group with which we interact. Consider the following simple process.

Listen/Observe

↓

Interpret/Assess (FACTOR)

↓

Check/Clarify

↓

Translate/Formulate Common Objective (FACTOR)

↓

Verify

The importance of ***communicating*** and ***hearing*** a clear and precise objective, relevant to the requirement and circumstance of all concerned, is crucial to successful gap bridging. Constant verification and clarification will keep the communication process on track.

An awareness of SPICE and REAP should be a reminder that communication is multifaceted and does not rely on language alone! When in doubt … ask!

Listening is a conscious effort to connect and acknowledge others

Seven tips to sound listening:[1]

1. Be relaxed and alert . Stress causes distraction.

2. Be silent. Allow others to speak; be *inwardly* silent.

3. Be present. Be at one place, mind, body and heart.

4. Be patient. Allow speakers to put their message across in their own way.

5. Go easy. To interrupt is to stop listening.

6. Ask questions. This allows for clarification and indicates that you are listening.

7. Suspend judgement. Avoid drawing conclusions based on partial pictures.

Be Respectful

- Do not be dismissive of others.

- Do not pronounce problems as unsolvable.

- Do not provide *quick fix* or flippant solutions.

- Do not *wash your hands* of situations.

Discounting or being discounted is harmful to self-esteem and results in feelings of isolation and inadequacy. Take care that non-verbal discounting is avoided.

---

[1] Source: anonymous.

Political Correctness & the Intelligence Process

The dynamic body of usage and custom that we have come to know as Political Correctness began as an awareness of and respect for differences between members of our own society and in the world as a whole. It is suggested that the term has since evolved to represent an *indefinable cloak of mediocrity* that denies the existence of difference and pretends that *X or Y* is the appropriate action for everyone to follow at any given time. The desire to appear correct often has more to do with how the individual, company, or society wishes to be perceived than with the people supposedly in need of consideration. Is Political Correctness just a *spoonful of sugar* that masks foul-tasting medicine? Is Political Correctness a mode that can be turned *on* and *off?*

To be truly correct, ask what can be done at any particular point in time to ensure that fairness, decency and respect prevail. Pause when the words *Zero Tolerance* are heard. Can this ever be a fair concept? Can absolute control be brought to bear without causing different inequities and prejudice? It is against this backdrop that intelligence must be gathered, shared, evaluated and acted upon.

Reaching different people at different times in different situations requires conscious effort. To ensure real *correctness:*

- Establish a common yet flexible goal.

- Factor yourself and others into the equation.

- Be empathetic and tolerant at all times.

- Respond to the person, behavior, and the words collectively rather than in isolation. Think big.

- "Do unto others as you would have them do unto you."

- Remember, failure to reach people is costly (SPICE, REAP, FACTOR, FERMA).

Any real change in life could begin only by example and the texture and quality being brought to it. Hence no one could take others further than he/she had taken him/herself...remember all men tend to become the thing they oppose. The greatest and most urgent problem of our time was to find a way of opposing evil without becoming another form of evil in the process...One had to reject corruption by *suffering* as much as corruption by *power*. ... The main sources of corruption in man, although there was a third, increasingly desperate contributing factor; corruption by numbers, our tendency to allow collective values to become man's greatest values.

- Laurens van der Post, *A Far-Off Place* (Recounting the ancient philosophy of the Bushmen)

The Written Word: Effective Reports & Correspondence

As a courtesy to the recipient, ensure that a document is as clear, correct and concise as possible. Intelligence correspondence should always be distributed on a *need-to-know* basis.

Positive answers to the following questions will indicate to you if your document (report, memorandum, note, e-mail, and formal letter) does the job:

- **Who am I?** The heading or letterhead should be clear; include your full name, position, contact numbers, and e-mail address, etc. where appropriate.

- **What do I want?** State your objective in the form of a ***Re: …. / Subject Line.*** As a courtesy to the recipient of the document, this information will ensure easy classification of your document. Remember yours might be one of many documents received. The document should comprehensively include the intelligence source, date and reference to previous correspondence.

- **Have I established relevance/benefit?** Your subject matter, your interpretation and recommendations should be made apparent as soon as possible. It is this detail that will result in the relevance of your intelligence being established. Have you established value?

- **Have I added any significant details that would raise flags, get attention, etc.? Have I conveyed significant detail about the potential application of the intelligence?** Take care not to *rewrite the encyclopaedia* - This information should back up the original premise/data/information and close the *sale*. Differentiate clearly between fact, information and opinion. Draw direct attention to any fears, ambiguities or uncertainties.

- **Have I called for action in an appropriate manner?** Use collaborative language at all times. Avoid prescription. The recipient will know that you are anxious for a reply or feedback. Remember: you are part of a bigger picture. Depending on your role in the collection process, a statement that you are available if required should suffice; you will be contacted if necessary.

Handy Tips:

- Work on a *what the analyst or employer needs to know* basis

- Be brief. Refer to, rather than summarize previous correspondence

- Avoid prescriptive, emotional, overly polite and sycophantic language.

- Do not lecture recipients on self-evident aspects of the project.

- Be collaborative at all times. When on difficult terrain, convey your wish to *explore possibilities and exchange ideas.*

The Intelligence Project Cycle

Intelligence procurement is not an exact science. As with all projects, goal achievement is dependent on efficient management of people, resources, quality, budget and time, all of which are subject to ongoing change. Flexibility and constant monitoring of the tasks are important if accurate and relevant intelligence is to be secured in line with set objectives. It is also important to be aware that, for external reasons, even the project goals might be completely changed or modified. Enough stress cannot be placed on the importance of simultaneous subjective, objective and big picture thinking (FACTOR).

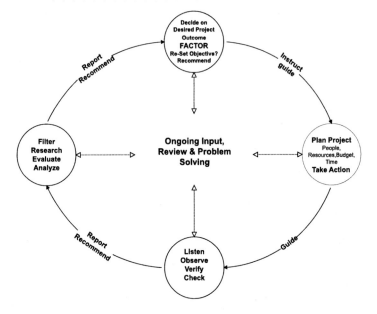

Figure 8.1: The planned project - Point Awareness.

The Intelligence Project

In the preceding pages, we have looked at what constitutes intelligence as well as a broad spectrum understanding of setting relevant and flexible objectives and pro-active decision making to better manage diverse personalities, people dynamics, and inevitable change.

Throughout the following simple process description, much of what has been written before will be repeated. This is an intentional part of the design of this book; we hope this will help the reader to tie theory to practice.

At no point is it intended that this methodology be adopted as a universal intelligence template. The content serves to provide a guideline that will enable the intelligence team member to evolve individual techniques and style that will result from independent thought and personal experience.

The following suggested steps will form the basic framework of any intelligence project:

Step 1:   Assessing Requirements & Defining Project Objectives

Step 2:   Planning the Project

Step 3:   Briefing the Team/Being Briefed

Step 4:   Securing Intelligence

Step 5:   Processing Intelligence

Step 6:   Recording/Inputting Raw Information

Step 7:   Forming the Intelligence Theory - Process & Analysis

Step 8:   Selling/Buying Intelligence Theory (Delivery/ Decision-Making)

Step 9:   Wrapping up

Step 10:   Cleaning up…Managing Security Risk

Individual awareness is the key to gathering, analyzing, recording and selling intelligence. Point Awareness and *Big Picture* thinking will always reveal the next step. Keep an open mind, stay focused, and be aware of

- The purpose of the project – gathering, analyzing, and processing intelligence

- How project success will be measured

- Project completion date

- Full use of people, resources, budget and time

- Quality standards

Step 1: Assessing Requirement & Defining Project Objectives

- Outline precise detail of what is required and why!

- Relate requirements to information already on hand. Place objectives in historical and factual context.

- Set up mechanisms to redefine objectives if necessary at some future point.

- Consider alternate objectives to meet the requirements.

- Evaluate the potential impact of secured or failed objectives.

This process is akin to deciding which missing pieces of a jigsaw puzzle need to be found. The more complex the intelligence scenario (requirement), the more strategy will be required to prioritize and define the information to be collected.

Step 2: Planning the Project

Set up guidelines or a flexible protocol to manage the project cycle. Consider:

- Scope and process to be followed

- Individuals and team composition

- Reporting timelines

- Reporting procedures

- Budget/Resources

- Level of quality required and the measurement standard

- Accountability and transparency

Step 3: Briefing the Team/Being Briefed

Accurately briefing the collector or collection team as to the specific intelligence required is a vital step in the collection process. The more detailed the brief, the more focused the collection and the less time and resources are wasted. (FERMA)

- Set out the project goals and specific tasks to be accomplished.

- Secure acceptance of individual and collective responsibility.

- Ask for input to assess any constraints or liabilities that may have been overlooked in the planning stage.

- Set up contingency plans of action to be followed in case of mishap.

- Specify channels of communication and reporting procedures.

- Divulge only as much detail as the team or leader needs to know to accomplish the set tasks.

Always check to make sure everyone concerned is on the same page. Recognize that diverse team life experience or culture will mean that different interpretations are put on words and concepts. Similarly, beware of passive personality types who nod agreement even when confused. More options considered and time invested at this point will prevent catastrophe and wasted hours or dollars during project evolution.

Step 4: Securing Intelligence

Specific Intelligence - The Open Project

An open intelligence project involves the analysis of selected information available to anyone. It is widely accepted in intelligence circles that most of the information (some say between 80-90%) required for production of desired intelligence levels is not secret and is readily available. The tendency in recent years has been to focus on expensive collection systems and to under emphasize evaluation of the source of information and analysis of what has been accessed. Reliance on technology has created the perception that a press of the button will bring forth everything there is to know on a certain subject. Tools are confused with product.

Important areas of consideration when setting out to secure intelligence from available or open information:

- The search and its objectives, if obvious to others, will in itself be intelligence for competitors, media, etc.

- Most information is raw in nature: it is not processed or placed in context of set organizational objectives and requirements. For intelligence to be *sellable*, the collector, clearly outlining value, and benefit or consequence, should provide comprehensive interpretation, including an evaluation of the source of information.

- The average intelligence worker is often neither trained nor prepared to filter information and provide intelligence that reflects diverse political, economic, social, national and international scenarios. This is especially true when the collector is faced with conflicting sources of information. Guard against the temptation to infer intelligence from available information. (FACTOR)

- Much has been made of the uncertainty of intelligence in preceding pages. For intelligence to be accepted the collector needs to be accountable. Since this is difficult to achieve with any degree of certainty, many collectors prefer to either water down their interpretations or withhold intelligence until in a better position to back it up with facts. This is dangerous, as valuable input may be lost. It is important that a corporate intelligence climate be maintained whereby whatever intelligence available can be confidently presented within a framework of uncertainty. The collector is ideally placed to assist the end user in this regard.

- Timing is critical in the intelligence business. The shelf life of intelligence is limited. A speedy initial report with regular updates is critical to keeping the ball in play. Decision makers require adequate time frames to run their own intelligence process.

- Competitors, the media and the public have access to the same data, statistics and information. The risk of presenting inaccurate and conflicting interpretations can be potentially embarrassing. Original viewpoints will be hard to come by if everyone in the first instance is mining the same source pool. This is especially true of Internet searches - a popular search engine will lead all searches to the same sites. Since the whole idea of gathering intelligence is to maintain the competitive edge, it is evident that securing distinct and accurate information is the primary objective.

Teams and their members must ensure coordination to ensure effective corroboration of information and to prevent unnecessary duplication.

Researching Intelligence

Use available resources; access in house expertise:

- Colleagues/colleague networks

- Industry experts

- Inter Departmental Liaison

- Industry cutting services

- Industry intelligence services

- Market research

- Commercial databases, industry journals and statistics

- Annual reports: competitors and suppliers, etc.; newspapers, magazines, books, and electronic newsletters; specialized electronic databases

- Trade associations, and government ministries and agencies, both international and national

- Related Organizations, Chambers of Commerce

The Internet

The advent of the Internet has brought with it the idea of a one-stop shop in the information-gathering process. Indeed the speed and convenience with which research can be conducted is unparalleled and vital in the communication, investigation and analysis of global events and how they impact locally.

It is suggested that the Internet be considered as *one* of many sources of information. If the Internet is considered representative of the world community then would it not also reflect human strength and weakness? Danger lies, however, in assuming that all Internet content is current, factual, and comprehensive. Similarly, be as varied as possible in Internet research avenues – avoid feeding repetitively at the same trough. Consciously break your usual patterns!

However convenient, it is crucial to remember that these sources are only as good as the input received. Be aware that even if a certain publication or writer has a good reputation and is generally well informed, the information at hand is not necessarily accurate. (SPICE)

Varied Source Research + Cross Reference = Probable Trend

Discovering Hidden Intelligence

Hidden intelligence is the information you discover at random when reading a given document or talking to someone:

- Keep *key words* conscious at all times. Contextual and lateral thinking will allow these words to jump out from the page as the document is scanned. Be aware of the value of developing the mental agility necessary to an exercise in cross-reference.

- Intelligence is not usually contained in headlines or lead articles or conscious statements. Look and listen for key words at all times. Often, a comment in a larger piece or a small article in the

inner pages of a newspaper or an unrelated
conversation will contain information about an
existing theory, point of view or trend.

* Societal trends may be read on political, economic
  or cultural levels (SPICE). Avoid limiting reading
  to a single area of interest.

* Develop a reliance on your sense of intuition.
  Trust your instincts. Do not be scared of
  uncertainty!

The Covert Operation

Covert operations involve the planned and secret
discovery of hiddent intelligence objectives. In essence,
the operation will involve searching for answers to set
questions.

Direct - Trusted Sources

* Every intelligence worker should have a network
  of reliable contacts.

* Ask direct questions that fall within the source's
  field of expertise only. A seasoned intelligence
  gatherer might well be able to disguise the reason
  for the question. Trust issues will arise if at some
  future point the source uncovers the real reason
  for the question. Be aware that any question will
  in all likelihood alert the person to your objective.

* Even with trusted sources, take care to provide
  only such detail as is absolutely necessary when
  asking for information that might reveal strategic
  information or objectives. Work on the *least said,
  soonest mended basis*, as sources can be
  compromised at any point in the relationship.

- Remember that every relationship is a two way street. See that the source receives due consideration and acknowledgement on all levels. (SPICE & REAP)

Indirect - Ulterior questions (fishing expedition)

- The trick is to find out what people know about a certain subject and to get them to talk without actually asking a direct question. Statements that are directly opposite to what the target is known to believe would be an effective example: an emotional or headstrong individual will almost never resist the urge to *put someone right*. Conversations about related topics can be skillfully steered to the matter at hand.

- Ulterior behavior requires skill and should be used only when strictly necessary. If the target sees through the ploy, at the time or later, trust will have been broken perhaps irretrievably.

Consider all information/data/statistics on individual merit: case by case, situation by situation, source by source.

Step 5: Processing Intelligence

Raw Information → Theory → Product

Eventually, a dynamic intelligence product will result from analysis, research, recording and updating of a potential blend of global, national, industry, organizational and random clues, assembled to form a theory that will illustrate the potential impact on an organization at any point in time. The awareness of this should remain at the forefront of individual and team thinking while evolving or executing their segment of the intelligence process.

Subjective Clues Discovered + Objective Analysis
+ Subjective Context = Relevant Theory

An intelligence theory, much like any other, is the result of a process that attempts to make sense of otherwise disparate facts. Ideas, concepts, models and plans are continually evolved to contextualize factual experience. In the intelligence world, we are concerned about this evolution in the light of the future events.

The distilled sense made of independent events, decisions, actions, people and circumstance will allow analysts and decision makers to commit to or reject a specific course of action. As is natural, diverse people will respond in different ways (REAP) to explanations, actions, responses, and ideologies that are put before them. Automatic modification and testing will occur in direct proportion to subjective experience and individual vision (SPICE) of the future.

In the ideal world, an intelligence theory will

- Be recognizable as a logical progression

- Consist of material facts and process showing cause and effect

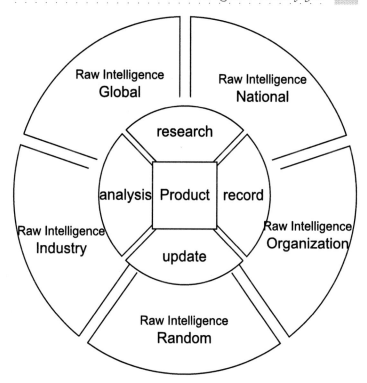

Figure 8.2: The Analysis, Research, Recording and Updating steps in the intelligence product creation process.

- Result from the specified input of the gatherer and analyst

- Clearly link opinion and recommendations to bottom line business or organizational objectives

Logically, alternative responses that include inaction, procrastination, or agreement and relevant action are to be expected. The element of thinking and individual choice is always present (FACTOR).

The *onus* is on each individual in the intelligence process to facilitate easy understanding of the material put forward. Faulty communication, misinterpretation, manipulation and the given psychological environment will always provide obstacles to the easy passage of any intelligence theory. Currently, the reliance on proven process and *what works* is the single biggest obstacle, in this regard.

To ensure that the theory is as clear as possible, theory formulation should strive to link the subjective conditions of the target audience, analyst, or decision maker with required duties, business obligations, or functions.

In larger organizations, theoretical impact is further complicated by the need for multi–person inter-departmental consultation, compromise and bargaining.

The Evaluation Process

A theory that shows a clear and logical evaluation of all its components and their origin will be the surest guide to ensuring that it secures the attention of the desired audience as well the objective consideration that it deserves.

Ensuring an accurate, mistake-free evaluation of an item of intelligence or source of information is a virtual impossibility. Acceptance of this fact would be the first step in the creation of a process that would allow for the rational evolution of a theory. Working with intangible future events is not an exact science! People naturally evaluate those that they meet and the information that they receive. In this line of work, it is crucial that this innate process be made conscious.

Evaluation of the Source

Using innate powers of observation and analysis evaluate the source (SPICE and REAP).

Your objective should be to build up a comprehensive, evolving picture of the person or media in question that will result in a determined effort to avoid inaccurate inferences, assumptions or deductions. Making facts fit the desired picture has been the downfall of many politicians, law enforcement officers and intelligence agents, often with disastrous consequences for others!

This is not a definitive process. A conscious look at the clues available will provide a balance of probability as to the integrity of the source and the information provided.

Evaluating Actual Intelligence

Evaluating information is even trickier than evaluating the person who provides it - the context or potential areas of relevance especially with regard to a large organization are so much wider. Intelligence and its connection to the organization will increase in relevance when shared with different individuals in diverse areas of the operation. The greater the organizational emphasis on knowledge sharing, the greater the chances are of ongoing receptiveness to vital intelligence. It is again stressed that the unknown will always be present in intelligence gathering, involving a certain amount of risk to any recommendation made post evaluation.

Cross-referencing is the most effective tool in the evaluation and processing of intelligence. It is important to remain focused on a set objective while thinking and keeping an open mind.

A simple organizational evaluation process would be as follows:

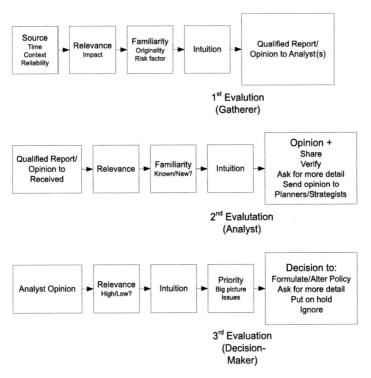

Figure 8.3: *A sample organizational evaluation process.*

Step 6: Recording/Inputting Raw Information

All intelligence should be indexed and classified for easy access. Ideally, the organization will have a generic system that will allow information to be filed and stored in categories that are common to the entire organization. Maximum intelligence accuracy will best be achieved by the existence of diverse, yet connected collection and storage points; input from different collection/process points will create an internal network that will ensure the making of more informed decisions. Accept the inevitable uncertainty of the process.

An intelligence operation is virtually useless unless it includes knowledge management concepts and capabilities that allow consumers to sort and process the available information. As has been seen on national levels, many organizations have obtained information and data at great expense that lies idly in costly storage banks. Although important technological developments are being refined to provide a greater degree of speed and accuracy, the intelligence analyst has not developed the capacity to inclusively distil and digest the overwhelming and often conflicting amount of information available. For this reason, it is vital that information be shared and made available across the corporate intelligence community. Ongoing discussion and thinking will allow full use of the intelligence available. The attention given to focus and big picture thinking in the preceding pages is of particular importance in ensuring a common corporate awareness of process.

Suggested *Awareness* Factors in the Input Process

- Organizational input/storage policy; efficient back-up procedure

- Indexing, tagging, and cross-referencing systems

- Integrated inter-departmental systems

- Soft and hard copy options

- Inter-departmental knowledge sharing

- Climate of debate and shared opinions

- Recognition of inconsistency or novelty

- Acceptance of the fluidity of the intelligence world

- Empathy and support for the Information Technology team – in reality, an Us vs. Them situation often develops with the end-user group. The IT team members are not miracle workers, but a group dependent on corporate budget and vision as well as input provided by colleagues.

- The IT team that invests in an open door policy, keeping decision-makers and budget administrators informed of priority requirements will make an enormous contribution to the efficiency of intelligence input and the consequent information flow.

Information Technology & Internal Intelligence Process

Information Technology is the tool or system in any given organization that increasingly (and in some cases exclusively) bridges the gap between the diverse players in the intelligence cycle.

The often awe inspiring use of technology in the process of information analysis is welcomed, but should be approached with realistic expectations. Care should always be taken to remember that information technology is an *extension* of capacity, not a *replacement* of innate human capacity to analyze. Similarly, it is also advisable to bear in mind that while any knowledge management system should be geared to compensate for human imperfection in processing and storing complex and vast amounts of information, individual decision making is a vital factor in the efficient use and updating of technology.

An efficient IT system will ideally:

- Reflect a system and key player structure that facilitates the capture, recording, processing and availability (information flow) throughout the organization.

- Integrate IT into the business operation and best practices policies.

- Allow for cross-referencing (e.g. interdepartmental), external input and review protocols.

- Clarify the basis for (limits of) the analysis provided.

- Clarify the level of exclusivity provided.

- Establish the degree of certainty with which the analysis may be relied upon.

- Demand end-user participation and thinking by providing alternative scenarios and requests for input.

- Facilitate and prompt for regular content updates.

- Use IT applications and cross domain transaction tools such as KCRM, Enterprise Application

Integration (EAI) systems that enable the simultaneous interfacing of different CRM and CI programs.

- Maximize the security capabilities of all software to reduce demands on IT administrators.

- Have security tools, functions and settings that are simple to implement and easy to use.

Today, numerous vendors produce diverse offerings that tend to be quite complex due to the variety of disconnected systems they pull together. To secure the right system, evaluation must take place on a system-by-system basis in the context of specific business requirements as well as the competency of the actual end-user.

Successful implementation is reflected by a system that works, is simple, relevant and user friendly. The motivation of the general employee group to efficiently use technology is directly linked to their corresponding comfort at any given time. Many organizations consistently make false assumptions about end-user motivation, resulting in costly and inefficient technology implementation.

Current Technology + User Enthusiasm/Savvy
+ Awareness = Efficiency

Intelligence Flow & Collaborative Knowledge Management (IT) Requirements*

→ *Gather*→ *Input*→ *Process*→ *Access*→ *Input*→

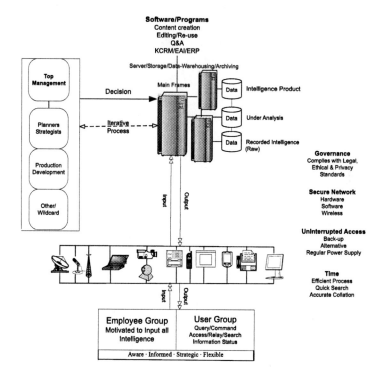

Secure · Fast · Inclusive · Accessible
Dynamic · Simple · Reliable

Figure 8.4: A view of requirements for the flow of intelligence and knowledge within an organization.

Intelligence & Digital Records

Authenticity

It is ***important*** to remain aware that technology has long existed whereby recorded documentation, photographs, etc. may be retroactively altered, inserted and expunged without a trace.

The lack of recorded evidence or even existing official records is not always conclusive proof that an event did or did not take place

The Digital Wasteland

As time passes, the durability and efficiency of electronically recorded data has been seen to be less than perfect. The intelligence worker should be vigilant at all times that the lack of information available digitally might be due to human or technical mishap:

- Poor records management policy and implementation

- Inadvertent deletion

- Incorrect *saving* of data (location/format)

- Unavailability or obsolescence of hardware and software to translate records

- Electronic originals not preserved in an alternate format

Conversely, a constant awareness of these potential vulnerabilities should be maintained when inputting and storing gathered intelligence. Adequate back-up procedures should be regularly updated and secondary records should be kept to provide uninterrupted accessibility to the storage system.

Loss of e-records

The erosion of institutional memory in a digitally documented world is a real and increasingly urgent threat. It's like corporate or national amnesia. You can't remember what you did. You can't remember what worked well. If you don't know where you've been, you can't know where you're going.

Terry Cook, visiting professor for archival studies, University of Manitoba (*The Toronto Star*, 16th September 2002).

Step 7: Forming the Intelligence Theory - Process & Analysis

Analysis is best viewed as the preparation of a product for an end-user or consumer. In the same way that great care goes into the preparation of a product that will be usable, so too must careful attention be given to the processing of raw intelligence. The material available needs to be a product that is of potential use to the organization. The opinion or recommendation of the analyst must be *sold* to the next step in the decision-making hierarchy.

The ongoing danger is the temptation to *feed* the client what it wants to hear. In the corporate world, the end product might not be particularly welcome, but nevertheless is crucial to the survival of the corporation. To this end, the analyst, like the collector, has the difficult task of subjectively understanding the intelligence and then objectively evaluating its worth against a subjective knowledge of the organization. In both instances, this would entail a conscious struggle against the reflexive human tendency to infer or draw conclusions to reach a convenient point of finality. The risk of displeasure, rejection and even error will not deter a good analyst. As has been stated elsewhere in this material, the facts should dictate the theory - the desired theory cannot dictate the facts!

Guidelines to Effective Intelligence Analysis

- Avoid the quest for the final solution - it doesn't exist!

- Factor in and stay conscious of a corporate mandate (if any), existing intelligence, knowledge, policies and prevailing attitudes.

- Be aware of or ascertain the timeline available.

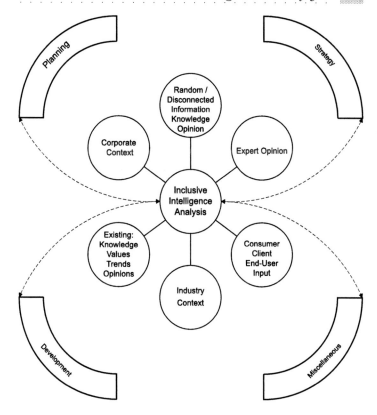

Figure 8.5: An analysis of the process for forming an intelligence theory.

- Create a delivery mechanism or model that will be understood by the organization, factoring in the corporate structure and the mind-set of the decision makers.

- Allow for varying levels of knowledge in the organization.

- Provide guidelines showing potential organizational relevance.

- Concentrate on the *gist* (core message) or broad framework in the first instance.

- Consider a system whereby an incomplete product is delivered (piecemeal), with a clear explanation, as and when available. This will allow for broader and quicker organizational cross-reference.

- Ensure the facility of further analysis and interpretation of the product elsewhere in the organization. IT solutions may exist for cross referencing.

- Make supporting detail available upon request.

- Provide corroboration from known or proven experts.

- Access input from other areas of collection and analysis that potentially will assist in subjective corroboration or re-evaluation.

- Monitor the process, remain flexible, and embrace change as a constant.

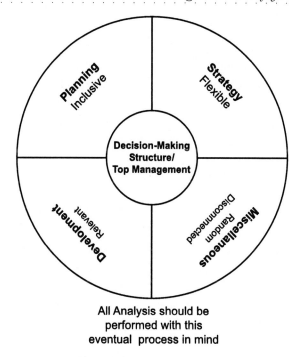

All Analysis should be
performed with this
eventual process in mind

Figure 8.6: Factors in the intelligence forming process.

Quantifying Probability: *Thomas Bayes' Theorem of Probability*

Conducting analysis of intelligence takes place in the random realm of uncertainty. Any conclusion drawn will at best be described as probable; selling the *probable* to strategists, planners and top management is a tough task. Interestingly, there exists a mechanism that will assist in determining the most probable scenario as well as bringing a quantifiable element into the equation for the benefit of those demanding a tangible degree of certainty - **Thomas Bayes' Theorem of Probability.**[1]

Bayes, an English Theologian and mathematician who lived in England from 1702-1761, is possibly the first person to have linked probability to logical process by providing a mathematical basis to infer probability. Simply put, he believed that by calculating the number of times a certain theory is put forward by experts, one could infer the probability of its actual occurrence. He pitted the known against the unknown! This approach, he felt, would allow experts to make use of knowledge they did not know they had – a big picture approach to analysis:

- Brainstorm to evolve a short list of possible scenarios that might be dictated by the newfound intelligence.

---

[1] $P(H/E, C) = P(H/C) \, P(E/H, C) \, / \, P(E/C)$

The left hand side of the equation is known as the posterior probability. It represents the probability of a hypothesis H when given the effect of E in the context of C. The term $P(H/C)$ is called the prior probability of H given the context of C by itself. The term $P(E/H, C)$ is known as the likelihood. The likelihood is the probability of E assuming that H and C are true. Lastly, the term $1 \, / \, P(E/C)$ is independent of H and can be seen as a scaling constant. Cf. www.mrs.umn.edu

- Gather the group of experts to develop probable case studies for each scenario.

- As a group, repeatedly vote to narrow down the choice to arrive at a most probable scenario.

This will result in expert minds using both their rational expertise as well as innate intuition, forcing a creative draw on a wealth of disconnected knowledge that will possibly be of relevance to the situation at hand.

An interesting use of the theorem may be seen in a study of submarine espionage during the cold war.[2] Both U.S. and Soviet submarines went missing without explanation, resulting in multi-million dollar search expeditions all conducted with utmost secrecy. John Craven a U.S. Naval Intelligence trouble-shooter would formulate several hypotheses as to what could have happened and then collaborate with expert mathematicians to construct a map of the sea bottom. This done, he would repeatedly ask them to place bets on the probability of alternative scenarios – each a potential location of the missing sub. Using Bayes' formula he narrowed data down to *most probable* and plotted maps that were ridiculed as "insane" and "impossible" – yet he was always spot on!

Bayes & Information Technology:

Input of mass data/information→ Develop scoring system to map information→ Evolve theory→ Calculate key-word frequency counts→ Predict outcomes:

Past time trend analysis→ High performance forecasting

---

[2] *Blind Man's Bluff: The Untold Story of American Submarine Espionage* by Sherry Sontag & Christopher Drew.

Prediction of Outcomes = Competitive Advantage

All data should be analyzed in terms of the product used: ERP, CRM, etc. For example, technology that has the capacity to store infinite amounts of SKUs (stock-keeping units) is able to predict the sales volume of each SKU at multiple locations, producing forecasts in a matter of minutes (such systems have the capacity to analyze millions of records per minute). This forecast can then be factored into the specific supply chain.

Modern Day Application of Bayes' Theorem

Anti-Spam Technology

In 2002, Paul Graham[3] described in an article called *A Plan for Spam* how he cleverly developed an algorithm using the Bayes' Theorem to determine the likelihood of a word being considered *spam* by considering how likely any given word or Internet feature would be used in a spam message.

The likelihood of future use of a word is based on the number of times it was identified as spam in the past. This means that the more spam that is generated and identified as such in relation to legitimate messages, the higher the odds that future spam will be identified. For example, if the words *Enhance* and *member* appear in a hundred spam messages and only once in a normal message then there is a 99% chance of an e-mail containing these words being considered spam by a spam filter. All spam filters are programmed to have a tolerance level that will reject a message with a certain word count.

---

[3] www.paulgraham.com/spam or www.process.com/precisemail/bayesian_example

It is clear that this is a very dynamic process, dictated by what end-users consider spam – a blend of human and technical interaction. The example mirrors exactly the intelligence process: identifying probable future industry trends, threats, market preferences, and client or consumer attitudes all based on what has happened in the past.

The kicker here is to remember that the process is constantly changing. Much like a data base, it is only as good as its last update and the mindset of the person accessing its content. The inherent danger of human laziness abdicating the thought process to technology is ever present.

Step 8: Selling & Buying Intelligence Theory (Internal)

Communicating the processed intelligence product to the policy maker is a sale. The product will have a potential end use for the policy maker; it is the task of the analyst to sell relevance or benefit to the product to the policy maker. (See the section on Making Content Work)

- Any insights the analyst has regarding style, personality, mood, interests or preferred communication media should be factored into the equation (SPICE). Similarly, any personal baggage or history that the analyst may have accumulated with the decision makers should be considered. Decide on the best person or vehicle to deliver the recommendation - know the client!

- A well defined objective (FACTOR) is essential. The situation where the policy maker has to guess at any aspect of your recommendation is tantamount to a roll of the dice and a waste of the time and effort that went into the collection and analytical process.

- Effective communication (FERMA) will result in dialogue from which both the analyst and policy maker will be able to learn more about the process and enrich the corporate knowledge base. Challenges in the *sale* process should be noted to better handle future interaction in the future. Recognition of prevailing human and technical limitations will result in a more flexible and collaborative approach to the process. An effective communication will be reflected by a relatively straightforward message that will result in action.

At this point in the intelligence cycle, as always, the information provider has to step back and draw a fine line between handing over responsibility and ensuring the ongoing use and integration of the product.

- Fact/Information + Context + Interpretation/ Prediction = Intelligence

- A Well Defined Intelligence Product + Effective Communication = Effective Policy Input

- Effective Policy Input + Collaborative Discussion = Dynamic Intelligence Cycle

---

The moving finger writes; and, having writ,
Moves on; nor all thy piety nor wit
Shall lure it back to cancel half a line,
Nor all thy tears wash out a word of it.

Omar Khayyam

Suggested Report Document Structure

Classification

(Top Secret, Secret, Confidential, Classified, Priority, Urgent)

To:

From: *(Full name, position and contact details)*

Date:

Re: *(Subject matter using readily recognizable title that fully describes content)*

Previous Correspondence:
Your file #: xxx   Title: yyy   Dated: zzzz
My file #: xxx   Title: yyy   Dated:zzzz

Content:

- A short factual account that will unambiguously draw attention to the issue, information and data under discussion as well as the source, time and place of collection.

- Contextual setting of the intelligence and source as per the collector or analyst.

- The perceived relevance of the intelligence; and potential organizational consequence.

- Clear expression of perceived accuracy, level of corroboration, misgivings, doubts, degree of completion at time of writing, etc.

- Recommendation.

- Call for action, where appropriate; clearly indicating time constraints.

- Intended follow-up date.

Close:

> • State any pending activity; and indicate availability to provide further detail.

Strive for human interaction in the Intelligence Cycle. People are more inclined to describe verbally what they are unable (or lack the confidence) to write. Direct contact allows for a greater use of SPICE.

Building Trust with Decision Makers

Selling the policy maker on the value of specific intelligence should not be confused with imposing inaccurate information or working to a hidden agenda.

Building trust with decision makers is important because they will always need to know why they have (are expected) to act on recommendations received. The reputation the analyst enjoys with those making decisions will greatly facilitate the sale of the new intelligence theory. Reputations and relationships are not built in a day. It is important that ongoing contact and reliable service over a period of time will inspire the confidence and trust required to lessen the time spent overcoming resistance due to any of the factors that will potentially impede rapid intelligence flow. It is for this reason that considerable attention will be given to objective setting and effective oral and written communication in the pages that follow.

It is also important to remember that new intelligence might call into question previous decisions made, resulting in embarrassment for the person responsible. Trust and an empathetic communication style will help you ensure that an insecure decision maker saves face in situations like this. Being proven right might be exhilarating in the short term, but may have catastrophic effects when the next decision has to be made.

Lobbying & Influence – The Pre-emptive Sale

As part of an ongoing internal strategy, analysts in building relationships should consider the value of lobbying in their interaction. Lobbying refers to the preparation necessary to prepare an individual or group for a specific course of future action. The process would heighten awareness of how the land lies in specific areas – giving a strong indication of how receptive each would be to collecting, analyzing, or receiving specific intelligence. In other words relevant parties would be prepared or familiarized with the impact of intelligence before actually being required to do so.

Hectic schedules and diverse commitments often prevent decision makers from perceiving the urgency of intelligence at any given time. If the sale part of the process has been initiated prior to delivery, the importance of immediate attention/decision making will be immediately apparent.

Insistence on Relevance & Consequence – The Second Attempt

Much depends on the drive or determination of those selling intelligence theories. Non-quantifiable or non-rational theories might well be initially dismissed as fortuitous.

Intelligence rejection should not deter insistence on relevance if it is believed that what is offered is important to organizational well being.

Urgency itself is a concept that needs to be sold. Many decision makers will immerse themselves in discussion and requests for further information to avoid coming to a firm conclusion and deciding on a course of action. Inertia and procrastination should be recognized as normal barriers to decision making in direct proportion to the risk and perceived lack of consequence.

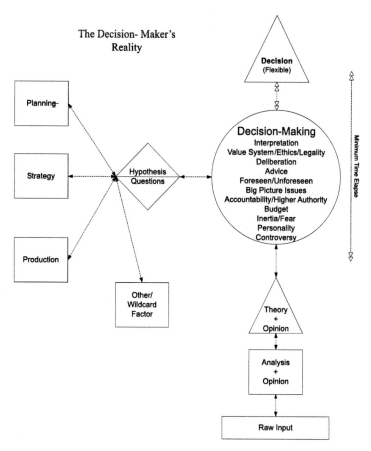

Figure 8.7: The decision maker's reality.

An awareness of the decision maker's dilemma will ensure a conscious individual responsibility to the steady flow of *on time* intelligence. Resistance, inertia and procrastination will be expected and dealt with. In turn, decision-makers would do well to encourage organizational *thinking* that embraces uncertainty and interpretation. Intelligence gathering and processing then becomes a conscious part of organizational life.

People experience things individually, according to their faculties and capacities. These things are like when people drink water and know for themselves whether it is cool or warm: it is necessary to attain knowledge on your own …a grain, then another grain, from vagueness to clarity. Each grain has a grain's power.

"The Secret of the Golden Flower" in *The Classic Chinese Book of Life*

Step 9: Wrapping up

Recording Project Procedure

Storing secret or classified intelligence is wasteful if it serves no purpose. Sharing certain information within a network of trusted networks, academic institutions, and businesses will allow for the evolution of common intelligence objectives that will include those who are already in the know and allow for a united and cost-effective intelligence campaign.

In the interest of saving time and money, and in order to simplify future research and ensure continuity, it would be helpful leave a *procedural map* outlining specific steps followed in a specific case. A simple and measurable outline could be created using **SOARR:**

- **Situation**

    - Circumstance; required intelligence

- **Objective**

    - Assigned duties and responsibilities

    - Project parameters (scope, time, budget, available resources)

- **Action**

    - Steps taken

    - People, resources, web sites, technology

    - Sources, places, organizations

    - Process - Analysis - Strategy

- **Recommendation**

    - Predictions, with reasons

    - Potential policies/solutions/strategies, with reasons and possible outcomes

- **Result**

    - Eventual use/policy

    - Outcomes

    - Measurable Success - Process/policy

Knowledge of History provides understanding, not absolute truth!

Paradoxically, it is important to maintain an awareness of the danger inherent in downloading the procedure map of a previous project in its entirety. Future requirements, players and circumstance are sure to be different. The tendency of a lazy or busy mind to follow an existing template would severely hamper the collector's ability to bring creative talents to bear and risk the oversight of hidden intelligence. Similarly, the emergence of an organizational *modus operandi* would become apparent in time to both internal and external observers.

A creative mind will look at a template for inspiration and guidelines while remaining flexible to accommodate people and situational dynamics.

Fresh Eyes…A problem shared, a problem halved?

Consider every time you have sought advice while engaged on important daily projects: while putting the final touches to a meal, winding up a decorating project, selecting a restaurant for an important occasion or agonizing over a crossword puzzle, how often has someone provided advice that has been akin to the last piece of the puzzle falling into place?

In the workplace, or when involved in something that has required hard work, original thought has a lot riding on the outcome: it is much more difficult to relinquish ownership of an idea, theory, *modus operandi* or project. In intelligence gathering, this is especially valid. One has to manage not only ego, but also the ever-present *need to know* rule. Asking an opinion may well reveal the intelligence objective as well as any intelligence gleaned. For this reason, great emphasis is placed on managing the unknown in terms of the SPICE model in Chapter 2. Risk is an essential part of the Intelligence process. At any point, the use of FACTOR should allow for a rational decision as to whether assistance, within *need to know* parameters, should be sought.

The advantages of securing fresh input can be dramatic. A good illustration can be seen by again looking at the decoding of the Nazi ENIGMA encryption system during WWII. Decoding involved person-years of repetitive and arduous processes of elimination to determine enemy communication codes that changed every month. Alan Turing and his team bore the brunt of this enormous task working in conditions of utmost secrecy. Understandably, the advent of freshly recruited mathematical minds resulted in a reluctance to risk sharing hard earned knowledge, yet it was one of the newcomers who quickly spotted a short cut (hugely cutting the decryption time) that had been missed by the exhausted eyes of the original team.

The ENIGMA saga further serves to illustrate the advantage of information sharing: making the decryption process available to the United States as opposed to decrypted intelligence allowed for technical improvements and an increased supply of decoding machines that again drastically reduced the duration of the decryption process. British fears relating to protection of intelligence gathering procedures, loss of *ownership* by individuals who had created what was described as *the work of genius*, as well as feelings of national pride were weighed against the advantage of being able to save more lives and ultimately win the war.

Calculated risk and trust in the face of a greater requirement is perhaps an unwritten law in intelligence circles. It is an open secret that the network of national secret services the world over is a resource to nations facing global issues. So too in the corporate world, where rapid company, industry or national advantage may be the reward for circumspect sharing of information and requests for assistance.

Using the Intelligence Product - Information Sharing & Internal liaison

Sharing information on a *need-to-know* basis encourages the continued climate of intelligence awareness throughout an organization. Management often balks at the thought of the work involved in widespread internal information campaigns and a potential stampede of intelligence activity. They are right... if the process is not well managed!

A corporate policy factoring in a constant change dynamic will appreciate an end-user requirement for regularly updated intelligence that will keep the organization operating at maximum efficiency. Judicious inclusion of the entire workforce in the gathering and dissemination process generates renewed intelligence input that in turn makes for a healthy learning environment. The resulting policy direction will be current and flexible, inspiring initiatives that sustain relevant and competitive results.

Information Sharing + Continued Input =
Renewed Intelligence Cycle + Updated Policy

Knowledge Sharing & Group Creativity Sessions

It might be advantageous to consider convening creativity sessions to mine potential innovation from relevant in-house individuals. Accessing knowledge or expertise that people are not aware they possess (the Bayesian approach) is the overall guiding purpose of this exercise. Sharing intelligence should be undertaken with three goals in mind:

1. Establishing an understanding the nature of the problem

2. Exploring the group's potential for input, elaboration, creativity, and innovation

3. Assisting in the group's future use of the intelligence

A strong facilitator, ideally the project leader, will be able to harness the group's creativity. But the variable that can be most influenced is the group's overall understanding of the problem. The ability to convey the project scenario, objectives, action plan, evolution and results will enable the group to apply fresh thinking and the generation of creative ideas for the experience.

Group Dynamics

While group composition will vary based on the specific project, there are a few basics that the session leader should follow:

- Ideas from all participants must be evaluated equally.

- As much expert diversity as possible should be included in the group.

- Clearly define individual roles according to expertise, while allowing for flexibility.

- Ensure that a sharing (not dogmatic) tone is preserved.

- Encourage free expression while maintaining focus.

- Outsider inclusion should be constantly monitored for hidden agendas.

Updated Policy + Mined Creativity/Innovation
= Refined/Dynamic Intelligence

Evolution of Best Practice Policies

Integrating lessons learned

A vital element of creating a healthy intelligence environment is the ability to integrate lessons learned to enhance the level of service provided. Internally, a knowledge culture that shares information will save considerable time and money, especially in the context of corporate knowledge retention (avoidance of a knowledge void resulting from attrition). Simple practical steps would be

- Gearing the company information management system to allow efficient access to a record of lessons learned.

- Officially considering integration of proven data, information, process, and technology as part of corporate best practice policy.

- Convening regular team forums to ensure an internal intelligence learning experience.

Example - Post Project Debrief

- What Happened? Accessing the lessons learned.

- Record details. (Ensure the ongoing safety of records.)

- Idea generation and evaluation.

- Build a consensus for potential process change/ improvement.

- Log and track the consensus.

- All team players are encouraged to identify training requirements as and when needed.

- Log and track effectiveness.

Working with internal teams and industry sectors will achieve a relevant best practice policy.

Developing an approach to gathering and processing intelligence that reflects outcomes filtered through the balance of probable occurrences will provide an effective policy. A quality product with ongoing access will ensure a high level of focus that will result in client satisfaction and interest.

Implementing this approach on a long-term basis requires fully-integrated intelligence process and a management system that requires a careful juggling of opposites:

- Details vs. Bigger Picture

- Structure vs. Creativity

- Certainty vs. Probability

- Discretion vs. Openness

Sharing Information + Identification + Evaluation/Learning process + Implementation + Adoption = Best Practice Evolution

A Current Organization + Innovation + Best Practices Policy = Competitive Edge

Sharing of information does not mean the abandonment of caution and turning a blind eye to the snooping competitor or media, but rather a shift of the intelligence mind set from:

Secrecy → Discretion

Control → Management

Updated Information/Policy + Managed Dissemination + Reaction + Corporate Intelligence Awareness = A Current Organization + Healthy Industry

Figure 8.8: A process to build a competitive edge through intelligence.

Unavoidable External Sharing & Best Practices

The information highway and IT revolution allow people to access pretty much anything that has been published. The ability to effectively absorb and analyze the available material is the challenge; hence, the preoccupation with *thinking*. The innate inability of the individual to innovate when stimulated is as important now as ever before. A Best Practices Policy exposing the individual to relevant information plus managed external industry and client sharing will enable a thinking response that will stimulate and corroborate innovation.

Measuring Project Efficiency Awareness: Tracking Time ... Saving Money

Much emphasis has been placed on the Point Awareness approach - thinking, setting objectives, and effective communication, etc. - which impacts on time in the intelligence cycle. It is obvious that time is crucial if intelligence is to secure the competitive edge at any given moment - delivering *just enough information, just in time*!

Table 8-1: Format for calculating the savings from an efficient intelligence process				
Task	*Daily hrs saved per person*	*Avg. billable rate/hr*	*Hours per project per month*	*Monthly project savings ($)*
Research / Knowledge Sharing	1.0	$100	20	$2,000
Communication: - meetings - email / phone - oral / written	0.5 0.5 0.3	$100	10 10 6	$2,600
Planning: - budget compliance - resource use - briefing	0.40 0.25 0.25	$100	8 5 5	$ 1,800
Instruction	0.5	$100	10	$ 1,000
Travel	0.3	$100	6	$ 600
Training				
Total team member savings per month			70	$8,000

The table on the opposite page (hypothetical data) is useful in illustrating the monetary importance of time awareness.

Recording Project Relationship Metrics

If it is accepted that relationships are crucial to successful intelligence gathering, then it follows that the intelligence process is strengthened by the input and analysis of *relationship data* that will enable the efficient planning and assessment of future project viability. The following examples are simple: consider the potential depth of like data recorded and the resulting capacity to plan a *best case* scenario.

Information Gathered / Provided	*Primary Source*	*Secondary Source*	*User Preference (Reliability Rate)*
Competition (New Product Initiatives)	Acme Publications	John Smith, Daily Gazette	John Smith
Customer XYZ (Loyalty)	Hazel Jones, Best PR Inc.	Industry Forecasters, Including Internet Research	Hazel Jones

Post-Project Individual Self Assessment – Learned Awareness & Strategic Project Value

Please ask and answer the following questions on a regular basis. Your responses are for your own information and will indicate residual value learned from the project.

Set an objective after each response for future reference if desired.

1. As an intelligence gatherer, analyst or policy maker, what areas of the company activity, besides your own, did you consider relevant to securing project objectives? (Tick the appropriate box.)

    ☐ Operations

    ☐ Sales & Marketing/Business networking

    ☐ Field Service/Customer Support

    ☐ Finances

    ☐ Contracts/Legal

    ☐ IT

    ☐ Human Resources

    ☐ Knowledge and support networking

    ☐ Social networking

    ☐ Other (please specify)

    On a scale of 1 (poor) to 5 (excellent), please indicate with a circle the degree to which intelligence awareness helped you in the execution of your project tasks?

    1   2   3   4   5

Learning Objective (FACTOR):

_____

2. How informed were you? Do you feel you have increased your general awareness of the company and its sphere of operations? Would you say you are aware of the big picture?

    1   2   3   4   5

    Learning Objective (FACTOR):

    _____

3. To what extent what do you feel that your Intelligence Awareness contributed to the corporate good or to project success?

    1   2   3   4   5

    Learning Objective (FACTOR):

    _____

4. How often did you formulate an intelligence theory from random information?

    1   2   3   4   5

    Learning Objective (FACTOR):

    _____

5. Would you say that, as a rule, you checked your theories with others?

   1　　2　　3　　4　　5

   Learning Objective (FACTOR):

   _____

6. As a rule, did you forward theories, data and information to relevant project members or other people in the company?

   1　　2　　3　　4　　5

   Learning Objective (FACTOR):

   _____

7. Did you allow others to be creative in all aspects of project execution?

   1　　2　　3　　4　　5

   Learning Objective (FACTOR):

   _____

8. Did you consider yourself as well informed in your field?

1   2   3   4   5

Learning Objective (FACTOR):

_____

9. Did others regard you as a well-informed *resource* in your field?

1   2   3   4   5

If yes, why?

_____

10. Did you receive random calls from colleagues or clients requesting information and sharing of ideas related to project completion?

1   2   3   4   5

_____

If no, why not?

_____

11. How good were you at researching requests for information? What media did you use?

1   2   3   4   5

Learning Objective (FACTOR):

_____

12. To what extent did you access personal or company databases?

1   2   3   4   5

Learning Objective (FACTOR):

_____

13. Have you written any articles, submissions, or letters directed at making an original contribution to policy or company wellness as a result of the project experience?

1   2   3   4   5

Learning Objective (FACTOR):

_____

14. Will you consider speaking at external or internal meetings? How do you imagine your ideas will be received?

      1   2   3   4   5

Learning Objective (FACTOR):

_____

15. How often did (will) you and colleagues passionately discuss the industry and related developments?

      1   2   3   4   5

Learning Objective (FACTOR):

_____

16. Did you enjoy socializing with colleagues (internal and external) during the project duration?

      1   2   3   4   5

Learning Objective (FACTOR):

_____

17. Did you consider yourself a big-picture thinker?

1   2   3   4   5

Learning Objective (FACTOR):

_____

18. Do you consider your thinking to have been a blend of logic and originality?

1   2   3   4   5

Learning Objective (FACTOR):

_____

19. Did you cope well with uncertainty and ambiguity?

1   2   3   4   5

Learning Objective (FACTOR):

_____

20. How well did you manage to stay motivated despite a lack of acknowledgement?

1   2   3   4   5

Learning Objective (FACTOR):

_____

This survey is not scientifically calculated but is designed to prompt an individual to assess his or her level of Corporate Intelligence Awareness at any point in time.

The questionnaire is for self-testing purposes only.

Add all the points in each circle to arrive at a score.

80 - 100 points   Excellent intelligence competencies.

70 - 79 points   Reliable intelligence skills in a time of emergency or difficulty.

60 - 69 points   Satisfactory - no risk to the organization.

50 - 60 points   Has there been a temporary setback in the operational area? Are you in quit and stay mode?

20 - 49 points   Awareness levels need a rethink! Are you in the right career position?

Keep an updated *objective* checklist handy. Use FACTOR to ensure focus and relevance in all aspects of the intelligence cycle.

Make conscious what is innate. Use all ability to the fullest. Be aware of why you make all decisions. Respond, do not react. **Live, do not exist!**

Step 10: Cleaning up...Managing Security Risk

Cleaning up brings the intelligence process full cycle. Just as caution was exercised in procuring the required intelligence, all traces of the analysis and process stages should be carefully removed. Failure to do so will allow unauthorised people to discover the importance of the intelligence to your organization. *Inadvertent indiscretion* could potentially jeopardize the hard earned competitive edge gained by hard won information – think of the cost in wasted time and financial outlay!

Concrete action

- Dispose of all notes, rough drafts, check lists and other paperwork once you have verified that all valuable information has been securely stored or recorded.

- Shred or burn sensitive documents, scrap paper, etc. The recycle bin or trash can is not the place for this material.

- Pay attention to reference material in your office or home. Books and magazines can tell an interesting story about a person as well as their interests, activities, etc. Check all documents for markings, underlining, and notes, making sure that no notes or other loose pieces of information have been left within the pages of any publication.

- Sweep your computers to verify that all temporary files, cookies, histories, and profile caches have been emptied. Do not allow just anyone to use work-related computers. Ensure that you use password protection at all times. Disconnect your computer from the network or internet when not in use. Log off and cut power when absent.

- Check with all colleagues involved in the initiative to ensure that they have taken similar steps.

Note: These actions should ideally be part of everyday routine. Understandably, this may be onerous at first but once in motion, it will not consume more than ten minutes of your day – a small price to pay for a more secure intelligence environment.

Intangible Action

- Put your ego on hold. Resist the temptation to be authoritative or "in the know" when the specific area you have been working with comes up in conversation. Your enthusiasm or level of knowledge might tip off a potential competitor.

- Associations, business destinations, and familiarity with certain events might be red flags to your competitor. Be circumspect in all you say and do.

- Again, the need to know rule applies. Proud family members often talk about their nearest and dearest – many business secrets are exposed this way.

Intelligence Awareness does not demand excessive secrecy, but rather a thinking approach to what/if/when information should be shared and ongoing mindfulness as to what the competitor might discover from your words, actions and interests.

CHAPTER

9

Summary

The Theory

- Information + Context + Interpretation = Intelligence

- Information + Context + Interpretation + Perceived Relevance = Useful Intelligence

- Useful Intelligence + Organizational Context + Benefit/Consequence = Relevant Intelligence Recommendation

- Relevant Intelligence Recommendation + Organizational Impact + Industry Context = Effective Policy Adjustment

The People & Process

- Impulse + Question + Subjective & Objective Awareness = Relevant Objective

- FACTOR = Relevant Objective

- Relationships + Openness + Awareness = Preparedness for Intelligence Gathering

- Preparedness + Varied Source Research + Conscious Cross Reference = Probable Trend

- Probable Trend + Analysis + Cross Reference =Well Defined Product

- A Well Defined Intelligence Product + Effective Communication = Effective Policy Input

- Effective Policy Input + Collaborative Discussion = A Dynamic Intelligence Cycle (DIC)

- DIC + Information Sharing + Continued Input = Renewed Intelligence Cycle = Current Organization (Updated Policy)

The Result

- Uncertainty Demystified + Conscious Thinking + Leadership + Ripple Effect = Corporate Intelligence Awareness (CIA)

- A Current Organization (Updated) + CIA + Innovation = Competitive Edge

The Quest for Knowledge & Direction

It requires courage to streamline or abandontheories, thoughts and ideals and, in so doing, ensure the growth of the corporate knowledge base. The inflexible intelligence gatherer will be mired in an outdated and perhaps inaccurate informational trap.

The philosopher George Hegel (1770-1831) underlined the importance of understanding the historical progress of world reason by looking closely at human life, thought and culture. World reason, he said, is the sum of human utterances. He felt that productive thought arises from subjective and individual consideration at any point in time. The result of that thought is valid only for that person at that time. In other words, there are no eternal truths because circumstances and people change all the time. His theory is much like Newton's view that for every action there is an equal and opposite reaction. The following model is a useful illustration of the ideal ongoing intelligence journey:

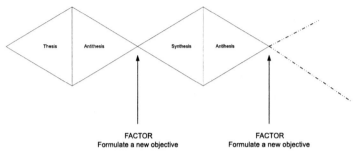

Figure 10.1: The ongoing intelligence journey

If the logic of this model is accepted, then it is safe to assume that managed sharing of information will result in the healthy and dynamic evolution of organizational intelligence and relevant, effective policies.

Use FACTOR to re-evaluate the ongoing premise behind the information or source as well as to set future objectives. This exercise will ensure continued input and a relevant contribution to the intelligence wellbeing of the organization. This is an ongoing process without end. Avoid being fixed within the framework of yesterday's dogmas and ideas.

Consider sharing corporate intelligence in the light of societal and national well being!

"Without contraries there is no progression."

William Blake, from *The Marriage of Heaven and Hell*

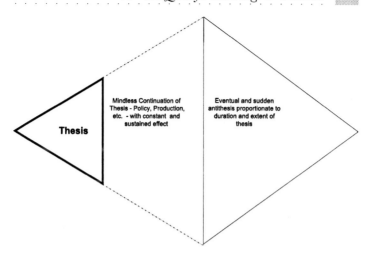

Figure 10.2: Hegel *Diagram inspired by Ben Jones, Director of Technology.*
(Vickers & Benson Interactive)

Unconscious continuation of an intelligence
thesis will, of necessity, result in an ultimate antithesis
requiring immediate action. Lack of preparation for
ensuing realities may be costly.

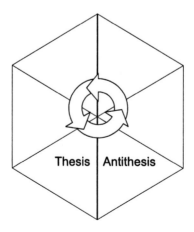

Figure 10.3: The thesis/antithesis cycle.

No conscious consideration given to intelligence evolution means limited horizons or expectations resulting in stifled intuition and lack of innovation with limited and temporarily safe results.

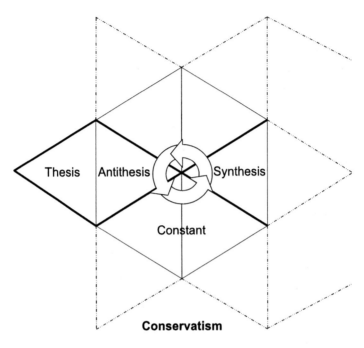

Figure 10.4: Without planning for the evolution of intelligence, much may be missed.

Given that change is an ever-present phenomenon, known intelligence frameworks only offer the illusion of certainty or safety - cause and effect is inescapable. *Marking time* and *holding pattern* policies or strategies serve to increase the eventual antithesis and necessitate a more dramatic synthesis. The variables are endless.

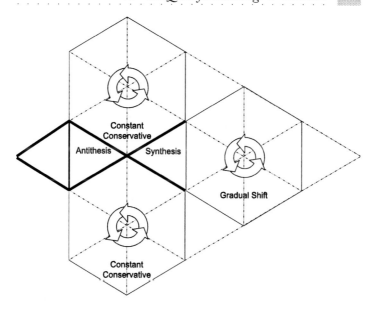

Figure 10.5: The result is an ultimate positive or negative consequence in proportion to the duration of the cause/input.

Be Aware!

Be Strategic!

Be Bold!

Be Decisive!

Be Accurate!

Be Insistent!

Be Flexible!

To place your ideas, your dreams, your desires before people, is to risk their loss…

To live is to risk dying…

The person who risks nothing gets nothing;

Does not grow, does not learn, does not love;

… Is a slave; has forfeited freedom;

One who is willing to risk not knowing the result, is free - unchained.

Go well into uncertainty.

Anonymous

About the Author

Rodger Nevill Harding
B.A., LLB

Throughout the 1980s, Rodger Nevill Harding worked for the South African government's Department of Foreign Affairs as a diplomat tasked with intelligence gathering and processing, as well as with making trade strategy recommendations. His postings included Paris, France, and Moroni, Federal Islamic Republic of the Comores.

In 1989, the South African government awarded him the the prestidgious **Star of South Africa** for meritorious service in recognition of his work in strategic international trade relations and development.

In the early 1990s, he spent several years teaching his techniques to South African diplomats and high level government officials.

Since that time, he has established a successful practice in Canada as a Business Leadership and Corporate Intelligence Consultant to corporations, organisations, institutions and individuals. He specializes in management, strategic opinion and communication, leadership, change, performance, and project and diversity management enhancement.

Web Site: www.HardingIntl.com
www.HardingIntelligence.com

Email: staycool@web.ca

Churchill's Adaptive Enterprise: *Lessons for Business Today*

This book analyzes a period of time from World War II when Winston Churchill, one of history's most famous leaders, faced near defeat for the British in the face of sustained German attacks. The book describes the strategies he used to overcome incredible odds and turn the tide on the impending invasion. The historical analysis is done through a modern business and information technology lens, describing Churchill's actions and strategy using modern business tools and techniques. Aimed at business executives, IT managers, and project managers, the book extracts learnings from Churchill's experiences that can be applied to business problems today. Particular themes in the book are knowledge management, information portals, adaptive enterprises, and organizational agility.

ISBN: 1-895186-19-6 (paperback)
ISBN: 1-895186-20-X (PDF ebook)

http://www.mmpubs.com/churchill

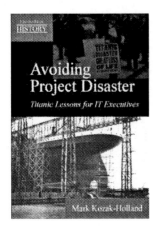

Avoiding Project Disaster: Titanic Lessons for IT Executives

Imagine you are in one of *Titanic's* lifeboats. As you look back at the wreckage site, you wonder how such a disaster could have happened. What were the causes? How could things have gone so badly wrong?

Titanic's maiden voyage was a disaster waiting to happen as a result of the compromises made in the project that constructed the ship. This book explores how modern executives can take lessons from a nuts-and-bolts construction project like *Titanic* and use those lessons to ensure the right approach to developing online business solutions. Looking at this historical project as a model will prove to be incisive as it cuts away the layers of IT jargon and complexity.

Avoiding Project Disaster is about delivering IT projects in a world where being on time and on budget is not enough. You also need to be up and running around the clock for your customers and partners. This book will help you successfully maneuver through the ice floes of IT management in an industry with a notoriously high project failure rate.

ISBN: 1-895186-73-0 (paperback)

Also available in ebook formats.

http://www.mmpubs.com/disaster

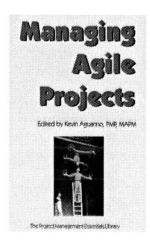

Edited by Kevin Aguanno, PMP, MAPM

The Project Management Essentials Library

Managing Agile Projects

Are you being asked to manage a project with unclear requirements, high levels of change, or a team using Extreme Programming or other Agile Methods?

If you are a project manager or team leader who is interested in learning the secrets of successfully controlling and delivering agile projects, then this is the book for you.

From learning how agile projects are different from traditional projects, to detailed guidance on a number of agile management techniques and how to introduce them onto your own projects, this book has the insider secrets from some of the industry experts – the visionaries who developed the agile methodologies in the first place.

ISBN: 1-895186-11-0 (paperback)
ISBN: 1-895186-12-9 (PDF ebook)

http://www.agilesecrets.com

Want to Get Ahead in Your Career?

Do you find yourself challenged by office politics, bad things happening to good careers, dealing with the "big cheeses" at work, the need for effective networking skills, and keeping good working relationships with coworkers and bosses? *Winning the Rat Race at Work* is a unique book that provides you with case studies, interactive exercises, self-assessments, strategies, evaluations, and models for overcoming these workplace challenges. The book illustrates the stages of a career and the career choices that determine your future, empowering you to make positive changes.

Written by Peter R. Garber, the author of *100 Ways to Get on the Wrong Side of Your Boss*, this book is a must read for anyone interested in getting ahead in his or her career. You will want to keep a copy in your top desk drawer for ready reference whenever you find yourself in a challenging predicament at work.

ISBN: 1-895186-68-4 (paperback)

Also available in ebook formats. Order from your local bookseller, Amazon.com, or directly from the publisher at **http://www.mmpubs.com/rats**

Need More Help with the Politics at Work?

100 Ways To Get On The Wrong Side Of Your Boss (And Strategies to Prevent You from Getting There!) was written for anyone who has ever been frustrated by his or her working relationship with the boss—and who hasn't ever felt this way! Bosses play a critically important role in your career success and getting on the wrong side of this important individual in your working life is not a good thing.

Each of these 100 Ways is designed to illustrate a particular problem that you may encounter when dealing with your boss and then an effective strategy to prevent this problem from reoccurring. You will learn how to deal more effectively with your boss in this fun and practical book filled with invaluable advice that can be utilized every day at work.

Written by Peter R. Garber, the author of *Winning the Rat Race at Work*, this book is a must read for anyone inter-ested in getting ahead. You will want to keep a copy in your top desk drawer for ready reference whenever you find yourself in a challenging predicament at work.

ISBN: 1-895186-98-6   (paperback)

Also available in ebook formats. Order from your local bookseller, Amazon.com, or directly from the publisher at **http://www.mmpubs.com/boss**

The Project Management Essentials Library

Managing Smaller Projects

"Simply put, this book is about helping people control smaller projects in a logical and effective way, and making the process run smoothly, and it is indeed a pleasure in achieving that goal."

IEE Engineering Management (12/04)

Mike Watson

Award-winning trainer and PM methodology guru

Not All Projects are Created Equal...

There is a dangerous gap in management planning and control. So-called "small projects" can have potentially alarming consequences if they go wrong, but their control is often left to chance.

The solution is to adapt tried and tested project management techniques. *Managing Smaller Projects: A Practical Approach* provides a low-overhead, practical way of looking after small projects that covers all the essential skills. From project start-up, to managing risk, quality, and change, through to controlling the project and implementing a simple control system, Mike Watson cuts through the jargon of project management. He provides a framework that is as useful to those lacking formal training as it is to those who are skilled project managers wanting to control smaller projects without the burden of bureaucracy.

We all run projects. The techniques in this book will let you manage them more effectively. As a bonus, the underlying principles are fully compatible with formal project management methods and can be integrated seamlessly into a corporate environment.

ISBN: 1-895186-85-4 (paperback)

Order from your local bookseller, Amazon.com, or directly from the publisher at **http://www.mmpubs.com/MSP**

Printed in the United States
55034LVS00001B/13-63